POOLEYS

PILOT AIRCRAFT GUIDES

Cessna 152

Martyn Blunden

Nothing in this syllabus supersedes any legislation, rules, regulations or procedures contained in any operational document issued by Her Majesty's Stationery Office, the Civil Aviation Authority, the Joint Aviation Authorities, ICAO, the manufacturers of aircraft, engines and systems, or by the operators of aircraft throughout the world.

Pooleys Pilot Aircraft Guides - Cessna 152

ISBN 978-1-84336-107-7

Pooleys Flight Equipment Ltd
Elstree Aerodrome
Elstree
Hertfordshire
WD6 3AW
United Kingdom

Telephone: 020 8953 4870
Facsimile: 020 8953 2512
Email: sales@pooleys.com
Website: www.pooleys.com

Author - Martyn Blunden

Martyn Blunden is the CFI at a Flight Training Organisation and holds FIC, IRI and CPL instructor ratings. Originally he gained his PPL in 1978, which preceded many years flying in that capacity with a fair amount of farm strip flying. Martyn has a great depth of knowledge of engineering and training, although not exclusively aeronautical as he ran his own agricultural engineering business for 15 years. For a number of years he was an advisor for engineering training at the West Sussex College of Agriculture and sat on the National Council for Agricultural Engineering Education and Training. He is a member of the Guild of Air Pilots and Air Navigators (GAPAN), which itself has a long history for contributions to the education and training of pilots. For the past 15 years he has continued to work with young people as a youth worker in his spare time, introducing them to flying whenever possible.

Foreword

Flying is an art, sport, pastime, pleasure and profession. It has different meanings to different people and for some just a dream. I for one fell in the love with flying at an early age after a short trip into the sky with a friend of a friend. Probably the way it happens for many people. Every penny was then saved to enable me to learn to fly at the local field, on Condors (a wood and fabric taildragger). Like many others I tried the RAF, but didn't get past the sergeant in the careers office "don't think you are from the right background old boy " sort of thing, which was still around in those days. British Airways at Hamble was of a similar attitude. With self-esteem a bit dented but still a great passion for flying I remained a private pilot for some years until I realised that my destiny really was as a professional pilot. I cannot deny it takes a lot of hard work to achieve and maintain a high standard but I still consider myself privileged to do the job I do. Dreams are often hard to realise and in flying we cannot escape the fact that it is costly. So, any way in which someone who is already in "the club" can help others to do likewise, even if it is just in the form of encouragement and valuable advice should be done with enthusiasm. As, I too was encouraged to write this book. There is nothing quite like a club room full of pilots for opinions! But out of that sometimes gems of wisdom do come. Flying really is an activity where one can benefit from the experience of others; my experience (apart from flying) lies in engineering. So I hope through the pages of this book I can pass on some of my knowledge that may help at some time. Also included is information that I have had passed on to me from my instructors in the past and that distilled from the flight manual. I hope that you find the information useful whether it be, sport, pleasure or professional flying you indulge in. I would also like to thank my partner Helen for her help in putting together the draft document and for some of the diagrams that accompany the text.

The Aircraft and its Systems

Having a sound understanding of "what makes the aeroplane work", will equip the pilot with a better knowledge to deal with any malfunctions should they occur in flight. Better still; spot a potential problem before it becomes an airborne dilemma. It is the intention of this guide to provide the pilot with the background information to assist in achieving the best and safest performance from the aircraft. Some basic engineering principles are also explained where it is thought appropriate, for the benefit of student pilots and those unfamiliar with the subject matter. Or, where a bit of revision would not go a miss!

However this document is not authoritative, as the only such document is the official Pilot's Operating Handbook/Flight Manual. Each aircraft has its own POH/FM that is amended for any single particular aircraft for variations in specification and country of operation. It is to the POH of the aircraft that you fly, you should consult, for operational procedures, performances and safety matters in the interest of good airmanship.

In addition to the a personal interest in how the aeroplane works, a pilot should also remember that in the UK the Air Navigation Order sets out in article 43 legal pre-flight actions required of the commander of an aircraft. This is reproduced here to remind us of our legal responsibilities as pilots even before we get airborne. Failure to comply with these or any other pertinent requirements could lead to legal prosecution should an incident or accident occur.

Article 43

Pre-flight action by commander of aircraft

43   The commander of an aircraft registered in the United Kingdom shall reasonably satisfy himself before the aircraft takes off:

(a) that the flight can safely be made, taking into account the latest information available as to the route and aerodrome to be used, the weather reports and forecasts available and any alternative course of action which can be adopted in case the flight cannot be completed as planned;

(b) (i) that the equipment (including radio apparatus) required by or under this Order to be carried in the circumstances of the intended flight is carried and is in a fit condition for use; or

      (ii) that the flight may commence under and in accordance with the terms of a permission granted to the operator pursuant to article 16 of this Order;

(c) that the aircraft is in every way fit for the intended flight, and that where a certificate of maintenance review is required by article 10 (1) of this Order to be in force, it is in force and will not cease to be in force during the intended flight;

(d) that the load carried by the aircraft is of such weight, and is so distributed and secured, that it may safely be carried on the intended flight;

(e) in the case of a flying machine or airship, that sufficient fuel, oil and engine coolant (if required) are carried for the intended flight, and that a safe margin has been allowed for contingencies, arid, in the case of a flight for the purpose of public transport, that the instructions in the operations manual relating to fuel, oil and engine coolant have been compiled with;

(f) in the case of an airship or balloon, that sufficient ballast is carried for the intended flight;

(g) in the case of a flying machine, that having regard to the performance of the flying machine in the conditions to be expected on the intended flight, and to any obstructions at the places of departure and intended destination and on the intended route, it is capable of safely taking off, reaching and maintaining a safe height thereafter and making a safe landing at the place of intended destination;

(h) that any pre-flight check system established by the operator and set forth in the operations manual or elsewhere has been complied with by each member of the crew of the aircraft.

So, to comply with article 43 we must also ensure all documentation relating to our aircraft is in order.

Documents that should be checked for currency and correctness are: -

Certificate of Registration
Certificate of Airworthiness
Certificate of Approval of Radio Installation
Aircraft Radio Licence
Noise Certificate
Insurance Certificate
Certificate of Maintenance Review
Certificate of Release to Service
Technical Log

This might seem a bit tedious and picky, but it is really just like any other pre-flight check. Remembering that the C of A is only valid if all the relevant conditions are observed and complied with (e. g. a correct check 'A' being carried out). If the C of A becomes invalid for a flight then the insurance will too. Although aircraft do not have to be insured by law, you would rather fool hardy to fly without it. Most aircraft operators would ensure that all the above documents relating to their aircraft are in order and that the aircraft are operated correctly, but mistakes can happen and ultimately it is the pilot's responsibility. And sod's law would state the day you have your little dink with an aircraft, is the day there is a problem with the paperwork due to someone else's oversight!

Therefore, we can see that there are certain legal requirements to understand our aircraft is equipped, operated and performs. However, hopefully in purchasing this booklet you are sufficiently self-motivated by interest or self-preservation to acquire a greater depth of knowledge of the aircraft you fly rather than to satisfy a regulation. If, at first, self-preservation is not a motivator then studying some of the accident reports provided by the AAIB may prove enlightening. Appreciating the limits of the aircraft's performance in differing circumstances and particular handling qualities will better equip the pilot to make the right decision in time of need. This may all seem a bit of "doom and gloom" and regulated but as pilots, when flying, we have a great duty of care to ourselves, our passengers and non-flyers below. That said, with knowledge rather than ignorance and hope, we can plan, prepare and take to the skies to enjoy our flying. End of lesson one!

Intentionally left blank

The Cessna 152

Principal dimensions:

Span	10. 11 m
Length	7. 29 m
Height (with beacon)	2. 59 m
Wheel track	2. 31 m

The Airframe

The C152 is semi-monocoque aluminium alloy construction. Which means that the metal skin is riveted to an underlying structure of metal frames, longerons and stringers. A well-tried and tested construction method dating from the 1930's. It is sometimes referred to as a stressed skin construction as the metal covering "skin" does indeed form part of the load bearing quality of the complete structure. It is a conventional construction for a light aircraft of its period. Some fairing parts, and wing tips are made from GRP. The high mounted wings are of semi-cantilever design with additional support from an external strut.

There is a 1° dihedral applied to the wings, which also have a small amount of wash out. The engine frame is mounted to the foremost frame and firewall. The firewall being a thin sheet of metal covering the frame and designed to prevent, or at least delay, fire in the engine bay from entering the cabin. The rear of the fuselage tapers to where the swept fin and conventional tailplane are fitted. To which the rudder and elevators are respectively attached. The high wing design affords a great view of the surface when flying but brings its own problems when turning in flight as a blind spot is created. The design also ensures that the aircraft is very stable in flight.

The C152 Instrument Panel

The Flight Control Systems

The Cessna 152 is fitted with full dual controls for pilot training. The control wheel or yoke is used to operate the ailerons and elevators through a system of cables and pulleys. Although the cables pass over a number of pulleys in the system, the action felt when checking the aircraft on the ground before flight should be smooth and with little or no resistance. Anything untoward should be checked out further before flight.

Ailerons

The ailerons are of the differential Frise type. A mass balance is fitted to the lower outboard channel section in the leading edge of the aileron, forward of the hinge line. Internal ribs are kept to a minimum and the skin is corrugated at three-inch intervals for strength. The ailerons are all-metal and are attached by three strip-hinges to the trailing edge of each wing. An adjustable push-pull rod connected by cables and pulleys to the control column actuates each aileron.

Elevators

The elevators are all metal with a combined masked/mass balance. Elevator stops are fitted to limit travel. The elevators are actuated by cable and pulley linkage to the control column.

Elevator Trim Tab

A metal elevator trim tab is fitted to the starboard elevator, actuated by cables connected to the trim wheel in the cabin. A position indicator on the wheel mechanism indicates the trim tab position. Forward rotation trims "nose down", reward rotation trims "nose up".

Rudder

The rudder is all metal with a fixed trim tab and rudder movement is limited by stops to 23° either side of neutral. Both horn and mass balances are fitted. Linkage is by cable, chain and pulley to the rudder pedals, which also control the steerable nose wheel. During flight the nose wheel leg extends fully, bringing a locking mechanism into place, which holds the nose wheel central and free from rudder pedal action.

Flaps

The trailing edge wing flaps are single slot fowler type, electrically operated by the flap lever mounted to the right of the engine controls on the instrument panel.

Flap actuation Control Lever

The lever is moved down through a series of "gates" to deploy the flaps in 10deg stages. When operated the flaps travel rearwards and down in a track which also allows a slot to open up between the rear of the wing and the flap. Compared to the simple types of flap fitted to some other light aircraft, the Cessna flap is very efficient at its job. Providing extra lift and drag when required.

An electric motor mounted in the wing drives another system of cables and pulleys to operate the flaps through push-pull rods. A sensor detects the position of the flap relative to the angle of deflection selected by the flap-operating lever and stops the flap movement at that point.

However, unlike a manually operated flap, where the pilot would feel a resistance to moving the operating lever at a high airspeed, there is no such feel in the Cessna. It is therefore quite easy to deploy the flap above the recommended operating airspeed limit of 85kts. This may cause structural damage to the aircraft and must be avoided by checking that aircraft is within the flat operating speed range of 85kts (Vfe) before selecting flap.

The Engine

Early 152's were fitted with the Lycoming 0-235-L2C engine up to about 1983, when the 0-235-N2C became the standard fit. They are basically the same unit, with some design changes to reduce the problem of spark plug fouling. It is a four-cylinder horizontally opposed air-cooled engine. The picture below shows the engine as seen from above with some of the main components annotated. In common with most modern car engines a large proportion of the engine is made from aluminium alloys ensuring a good power to weight ratio. Unlike a modern car engine however, is the lack of sophisticated electronic engine management systems that might lead to glitchy electronic problems. A simple type of carburettor and a dual magneto ignition system ensure excellent reliability. The basic design of a large cylinder capacity, slow revving engine fitted with simple ancillaries is more akin to an old style tractor engine than any modern car engine!

Top view of Engine

Engine Power

0-235-L2C   110 hp @ 2550 RPM
0-235-N2C   108 hp @ 2550 RPM
Full throttle static rpm (carb heat cold & mixture leaned to max rpm)
is between **2280** and **2380 rpm**
Cubic capacity **233.3 cu in. or 3.82 ltr**

The Propeller

A two bladed, fixed pitch McCauley 1A103/TCM6958 or 6950 propeller is bolted directly onto the end of the engine crankshaft. Minimum diameter 1. 71m, maximum diameter 1.75m. This gives an approximate ground clearance of 0.3m. During inspection the propeller is checked for damage to the leading edge, nicks and dents etc, and that tips are also undamaged. The propeller is a very sophisticated piece of equipment and even what might seem to be minor damage, can give serious problems if ignored. Poor taxiing technique or lack of observation whilst taxiing can easily lead to a prop strike on something like a taxiway light or even over rough ground. Or, a more extreme example witnessed at my local airfield recently, of an aircraft putting its wing into the spinning propeller of another, stationary, aircraft while taxiing! Needless to say, following the incident both aircraft required a visit to an engineering establishment. If a prop strike is suspected, then the engine must be shut down and a visual inspection carried out to assess damage.

The Engine Oil System

The oil system in an engine has to perform a number of quite arduous tasks that are not necessarily immediately apparent. As well as lubrication, oil aids cooling of internal components, removes by-products of combustion, provides corrosion protection and helps with the gas-tight sealing between the piston rings and the cylinder.

To achieve all these criteria the correct grade and type of oil must be used. Also the oil must be changed at the recommended interval time, as it gradually degrades in use and therefore, will not perform all of its duties correctly. Any engine manufacturer will lay down the specification of oil to be used in its engine and Lycoming are no different. Oil bought for a motorcar can vary massively in price for what may seem the same thing. The label of a cheap oil may state that it meets a particular required specification, and does so as it comes out of the can. Therefore, the purchase appears attractive. However, what it fails to mention is that the base oil of the product is of a low grade and will degrade far more quickly than a 'quality' oil. Hence, the sought-after protection etc for the engine will be compromised. An aviation grade oil ensures that the specification of the oil is still met after the oil has done its time working in the engine, maximising engine life.

There are two oil specifications listed for the C152, depending upon whether the engine is within its first fifty hours of life or not.

First fifty hours: MIL-L-6080 Aviation Grade Straight Mineral Oil.
Thereafter: MIL-L-22851 Ashless Dispersant Oil.

The different types of oil must not be mixed. As with all things in aviation, if in doubt about the correct oil ask! Both types of oil are available in various viscosities to suit different average surface air temperatures.

In the P. O. H. Cessna list the recommended oil viscosities for a particular range of surface air temperatures.

Example:
0-235-N2C eng. – *(New or rebuilt within first fifty hours)*
Temp. −1°C *(30F)* **to +32°C** *(90F)* **SAE 40 MIL-L-6082 Straight Mineral Oil**

0-235-N2C eng. – *(after first fifty hours)*
Temp. −1°C *(30F)* **to +32°C** *(90F)* **SAE 40 MIL-L-22851 Ashless Dispersant Oil**

The SAE number shown reflects the viscosity of the oil. The lower the temperature the lower the viscosity should be. However, usually the oil container will have the commercial viscosity grade number printed on it, which is approximately double the SAE equivalent. Therefore, the first example would have grade 80 Straight Mineral Oil. The second, being Ashless Dispersant Oil has a W prefix, therefore W80. Bearing in mind the confusion that might arise in the oil department, it is advisable to check with the maintenance organisation responsible for your aircraft which type and grade of oil should be used in the engine. They may prefer and recommend a modern multi-grade oil that performs well over greater range of temperature.

A Typical Lubrication System

The engine in the C152 has a wet sump (i. e. the oil reservoir is in the bottom of the crankcase). Oil is drawn from the sump through a gauze filter into the engine driven pump; this then pumps the oil under pressure to requisite parts of the engine.

Firstly, though, the oil is directed to the oil filter where particle contaminants are removed. If the filter becomes blocked then a valve will open allowing unfiltered oil to bypass it and continue round the system. This is only likely in the event of the filter not being changed at the correct service period. After the filter, the oil flows to the oil cooler, mounted in the front of the engine cowling.

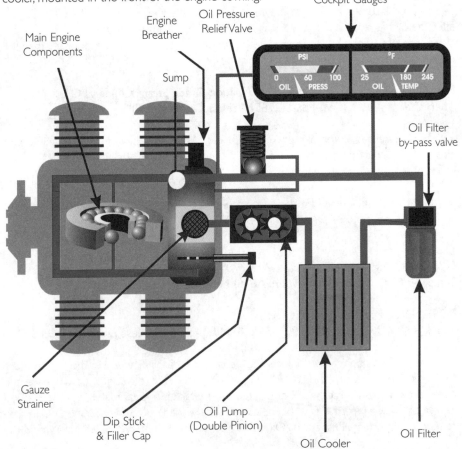

The oil cooler can be seen here through the front cowling looking like a mini radiator just behind the starter motor drive ring gear.

A thermostatic by-pass valve allows cold oil to by-pass the cooler, which helps the oil warm up more quickly on start up when the oil is cold. From here the oil is fed past a pressure relief valve and on to the oil galleries within the engine crankcase that supply all the various moving parts within the engine. The relief valve works by directing any over pressure oil back to the sump, bypassing the moving bits. One reason for ensuring the oil is at a reasonable working temperature before take-off, is that it is easier for the pump to generate over pressure oil with cold oil. Meaning that a reduced volume of oil is reaching the important parts of our rapidly revolving engine. When, more than ever, we wish the engine to carry out its task to the best of its ability! One good reason for having the oil temperature gauge that is fitted. A pressure gauge is also fitted and mounted alongside the temperature gauge on the instrument panel. Although, in common with most engines, this is only measuring the pressure at one point in the engine and with cold oil especially this may be quite different at another point.

Oil capacity: 6US quarts (min 4qts)

A couple of further points worthy of mention are. Firstly, following checking of the dipstick for volume accessed through upper cowling hatch, be careful not to over tighten the cap (especially when the engine is hot), as it may prove very difficult to undo. Secondly, as the oil drains back to the sump by gravity, it takes a while before an accurate reading as to the volume in the sump can be made, if the engine has been running.

The Fuel System

Normal fuel used is Avgas 100LL (coloured blue)
Also approved: 100 (formerly 100/130) (green)
L2C engine may use Mogas (i. e. 4 star petrol)

In the UK the CAA lay down procedures and limitations in an airworthiness notice that must be adhered to.

The fuel is stored in two wing tanks and supplied to the engine by gravity via pipework, shutoff valve, strainer and then the carburettor as seen in the diagram below. Each tank has an electrical level sensor connected to the gauges mounted on the lower left instrument panel. However, in common with most aircraft a visual check of the contents is vital, together with some form of calibrated dipstick to compare with the reading given on the gauges.

We can see in the diagram opposite that fuel flows from the tanks into a pipes joining both tanks to the shut off valve mounted on the cockpit floor between the front edges of the seats. The valve operating lever is normally left in the on position, lying horizontally on the floor. Moving the lever to the vertical position would turn off the fuel supply. Fuel then flows on to the strainer, where a feed is taken off to the primer pump.

The primer is a simple piston and cylinder type pump and is mounted on the lower left of the instrument panel. A peg and locking collar is fitted to prevent inadvertent action. Turning the operating knob to line up the peg (on the piston rod) with the slot in the collar will allow the pump knob to be pulled out. This fills the pump with fuel, which, when pushed back in will deliver the fuel directly into the cylinder head near the inlet valve. Normally 3 or 4 strokes are sufficient to aid starting but this does vary between types and also the ambient and engine temperature. When not being used for starting purposes the primer must be locked to prevent fuel being drawn through the system. This would cause an over rich mixture and rough running of the engine.

The fuel strainer is also fitted with a drain facility, which is operated by a knob mounted next to the engine oil dipstick. Fuel should be checked for water and sediment by pulling the control knob, which releases fuel through a pipe that is adjacent to the nose leg. A fuel strainer tube placed under this pipe will collect the fuel to be checked. Each wing tank has a drain valve that enables the fuel to be checked in a similar manner. From the strainer the fuel flows to the carburettor where it is mixed with air and fed to the engine.

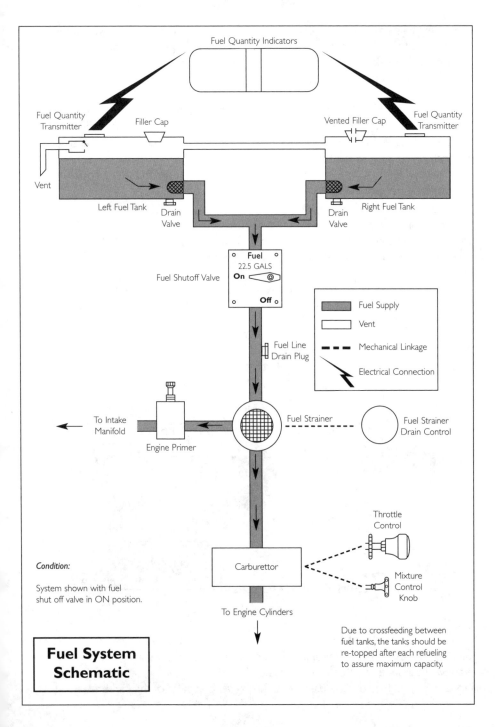

Fuel Quantity Indicators

Fuel Quantity Transmitter

Filler Cap

Vented Filler Cap

Fuel Quantity Transmitter

Vent

Left Fuel Tank

Drain Valve

Right Fuel Tank

Drain Valve

Fuel Shutoff Valve

Fuel
22.5 GALS
On
Off

Fuel Supply

Vent

Mechanical Linkage

Electrical Connection

Fuel Line Drain Plug

To Intake Manifold

Engine Primer

Fuel Strainer

Fuel Strainer Drain Control

Throttle Control

Condition:

System shown with fuel shut off valve in ON position.

Carburettor

Mixture Control Knob

To Engine Cylinders

Due to crossfeeding between fuel tanks, the tanks should be re-topped after each refueling to assure maximum capacity.

Fuel System Schematic

15

The fuel tanks are vented to ensure air can replace the fuel being drawn off by the engine. Two methods of venting are provided. Vented fuel caps and a pipe vent that can be seen behind the left wing strut. It is not unusual to see a small amount of fuel dripping from the vent pipe after refuelling.

A further point worth noting is that excessive or prolonged slipping or skidding manoeuvres should be avoided when fuel levels are low. As this could cause one or other of the fuel outlets to become uncovered and let air into the fuel system. Causing the engine and maybe pilot to splutter a little!

The Carburettor

It is very, and sometimes vitally, important to know how the carburettor and its controls function to get the best and safest performance from the engine. A carburettor is based on a simple principle, yet can end up as a very complicated piece of engineering. However, the pilot can still benefit from understanding how a basic carburettor works.

In the following diagram we can see a cross-sectional view of a simple carburettor similar to the type fitted to a Piper Warrior.

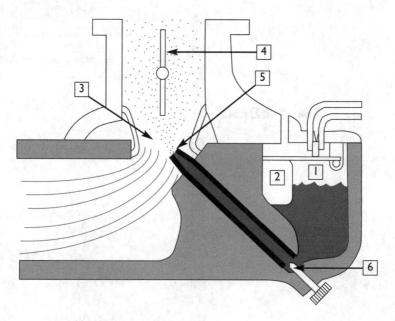

Fuel is fed from the strainer to the float chamber (1) of the carburettor. This is basically a small reservoir and the float (2) controls the fuel level by acting on the needle valve above. Basically a toilet cistern in miniature! In the body of the carburettor holes or drillings are formed to allow the passage of fuel to various parts of the carburettor. Air is fed to the carburettor by way of ducting to a central passage called the venturi (3). It is here that the mixing of fuel and air takes place. The air valve (4), or more commonly called butterfly valve, is connected via linkage to the lever type throttle on the instrument panel. This valve controls the amount of fuel/air mixture going to the engine by changing the volume of air that passes through the venturi. For the most part, fuel enters the venturi via the main jet (5) due to the low pressure caused by the venturi effect. When the throttle is in the idle position, it is virtually closed and there is insufficient airflow to draw fuel through the main jet. However, a low enough pressure is developed adjacent to the idle jet (not shown) to draw a reduced fuel flow through this jet. Fuel to both jets has to pass through the mixture control valve (6). This valve is connected to the red mixture control knob, mounted adjacent to the throttle, and is used to directly control the amount of fuel going into the fuel/air mixture. This control is also used to shut off the fuel supply to stop the engine. Stopping the engine this way attempts to ensure no unburnt fuel is left in the intake tract of the engine, thus helping to prevent accidental starting should the propeller be inadvertently moved.

The mixture control can be used in two ways: Firstly, to stop the engine by pulling the lever back and down to the fully lean position that cuts off the fuel supply to the engine. Secondly, it can be moved towards the lean position until a particular fuel ratio is achieved. This is discussed further later and termed leaning.

Finally, some carburettors are also fitted with an accelerator pump (8) and jet. This is also linked to the throttle so that when it is pushed in an extra amount of fuel is delivered to the venturi, ensuring smooth acceleration of the engine. C152's are fitted with this type of device from about 1980. Therefore a check of carburettor type is required, as exercising this type of throttle pumps extra fuel into the engine when you maybe using the primer as well. This runs the risk of flooding the engine, leading to possible poor starting and increased fire risk.

Fuel is fed to the carburettor from the fuel strainer mounted on the firewall. Air is ducted to the carburettor air box from either the front mounted intake filter, or a heat exchanger around the exhaust pipework (an unfiltered source). One version of heat exchanger is visible in the side view of the engine, the red hose ducts the warm air to the carb. Within the carburettor air box is a simple valve that is operated by the carburettor heat control knob mounted on the instrument panel that controls the use of warm or cold air supplied to the carb. Use of this is covered later.

The carburettor fitted to the C152 is known as an updraft type, as the air is fed into the bottom and drawn through to the top. The mixture then passes up through a tube in the sump that (when warm) serves a dual purpose. Firstly, the mixture is warmed slightly, which aids fuel vapourisation and secondly assists in oil cooling due to this heat transfer. Past this point the inlet manifold branches out to supply each cylinder with mixture through the inlet port and valve.

Side view of Engine

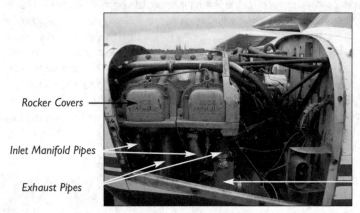

Rocker Covers —

Inlet Manifold Pipes

Exhaust Pipes

Heat Exchanger for carb heat

The Engine Controls

The Throttle

As mentioned before, this controls the amount of fuel/air mixture reaching the engine that in turn controls the speed/power of the engine. Rotational speed of the engine is displayed on the R. P. M. gauge mounted on the right side of the instrument panel. Normal idle speed is about 500-700rpm and maximum 2550rpm with a red line on the gauge to show this limit.

Maximum rpm obtained at full throttle will depend upon the engine load and airspeed. So, whilst you cannot "red line" the engine if stationary on the ground, it is quite possible to do so in the air. A friction nut is provided so that it is possible to lock the throttle or adjust its resistance to movement. Rotating the nut clockwise tightens the grip on the throttle and vice-versa.

The Mixture Control

This is used to adjust the ratio of the fuel/air mixture for optimum engine performance. The exact procedure is set out in the POH and is slightly different for each of the two types of engine and performance required.

There are various methods that can be used to achieve a desired fuel/air ratio depending on the instrumentation fitted to the aircraft. A complex type aircraft may have a fuel flow gauge, exhaust gas temperature (EGT) or cylinder head temperature gauge. However, none of these are fitted as standard to the C152, so all we have to work with is the RPM indicator when adjusting the mixture. For the later N2C type engine the procedure is as follows:

Set the throttle to give the RPM that will produce the power required at the cruising altitude currently being flown. This information is obtained from the cruise performance table (reproduced later in this section). Next, turn the mixture control in an anti-clockwise direction to reduce the fuel flow in the carburettor. Depending upon how over rich the mixture is, the RPM will slowly increase by a small amount and then start to reduce. At the maximum indicated RPM, by this method, the maximum power mixture will have been achieved. This is slightly different from the best economy mixture, which is used to generate the performance figures given in the tables. To accomplish the same performance the process, called leaning the mixture, is continued, slowly, after maximum RPM is seen and a drop of 10 – 25rpm is observed. At this point the best economy has been reached. Any further leaning of the mixture would be a false economy and would lead to serious engine damage. It would also cause the engine to lose power and then to run roughly, surely focusing the pilot's attention to the error!

For the L2C engine the rpm drop is 25 – 50. If the engine does not run smoothly or a sharp drop off in rpm is observed, as a guide, en-richen the mixture by about ¾ turn clockwise or as necessary to restore smooth running. Whilst flying the aircraft from the left hand side and with the rpm gauge on the right hand side, it is not always easy to see small changes in rpm so care will be needed when leaning the mixture to prevent over doing it. Therefore, this might be best practised on the ground first so that you are famil- iarised with the procedure needed to achieve the performance desired. Moreover, spark plug fouling can be a problem with some aircraft engine designs and using a correctly leaned mixture can reduce this.

Although we use the term "leaning the mixture", what we are actually doing is reducing an over rich mixture to the correct ratio. In the good old days! If you had a car with a manual choke, for instance a Morris Minor, and had driven the said car around with the choke out, which enriches the mixture. It would not be long before the old bus would start coughing and behaving like you were trying to run it on some kind of dodgy old moonshine!

Without getting too technical, the internal combustion engine runs most efficiently with a mixture of 1 part fuel = to 15 parts air (by weight) known as a 1:15 ratio mixture. The average aircraft carburettor is set up to give a ratio of about 1:12 at sea level as a basic setting. Efficiency aside, this aids engine starting and cooling. It also reduces the likelihood of pre-ignition and detonation. As well as efficiency, the fuel/air ratio also effects the amount of power the engine can develop at any given rpm. Starting to sound complicated? Well, now we will go and fly our aircraft to an altitude where the density of the air is much less than at sea level and complicate matters even more!

In the performance section of the POH tables show fuel consumption figures for various stages of flight. A sample from a POH cruise table is reproduced here.

Extract from Cruise Performance Table

PRESSURE ALTITUDE FT	RPM	20°C BELOW STANDARD TEMP			STANDARD TEMP			20°C ABOVE STANDARD TEMP		
		% BHP	KTAS	GPH	% BHP	KTAS	GPS	% BHP	KTAS	GPH
2000	2400	---	---	---	75	101	6.1	70	101	5.7
	2300	71	97	5.7	66	96	5.4	63	95	5.1
	2200	62	92	5.1	59	91	4.8	56	90	4.6
	2100	55	87	4.5	53	86	4.3	51	85	4.2
	2000	49	81	4.1	47	80	3.9	46	79	3.8
4000	2450	---	---	---	75	103	6.1	70	102	5.7
	2400	76	102	6.1	71	101	5.7	67	100	5.4
	2300	67	96	5.4	63	95	5.1	60	95	4.9
	2200	60	91	4.8	56	90	4.6	54	89	4.4
	2100	53	86	4.4	51	85	4.2	49	84	4.0
	2000	48	81	3.9	46	80	3.8	45	78	3.7
6000	2500	- - -	- - -	- - -	75	105	6.1	71	104	5.7
	2400	72	101	5.8	67	100	5.4	64	99	5.2
	2300	64	96	5.2	60	95	4.9	57	94	4.7

If we study the table we can see how much power the engine is delivering at a given rpm altitude and temperature. Although some of the differences may not seem too great, the significant differences are between the various % power figures and their related fuel consumption values. Applying this information to a typical cruise using the typical 2200 rpm setting. It can be seen that setting a higher than planned rpm, say 2400, can produce a significantly higher fuel consumption. Conversely, if was required to stay airborne for longer than originally planned, a lower rpm of 2000 will reduce the fuel consumption. Therefore, when planning a flight ensure you as the pilot are managing the engine to achieve the fuel consumption you expect! When to lean? Almost any when is the short answer. It is recommended when cruising at any altitude and using 75% or less power. It is permissible to lean for max rpm (i.e. max power) in the climb above 3000ft and will definitely be useful above 5000ft. However for most local and short navigation flights leaning could be left until established in the cruise phase. As mentioned previously an overlean mixture is undesirable, due to the reduced cooling provided by the mixture and the on set of detonation, which will destroy the engine. With this in mind any change in operating conditions (i.e. power setting or altitude) will require a resetting of the mixture control.

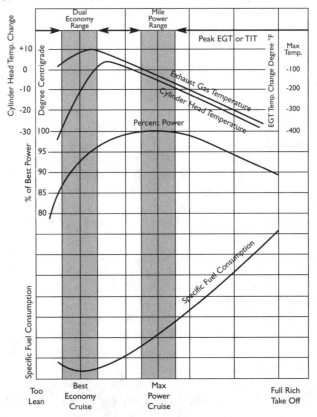

Carburettor Heat Control

To facilitate the removal and prevention of carburettor ice, a system that can supply warm air to the carburettor is fitted. A heat exchanger that is wrapped around the exhaust system is connected via a simple flap valve to the carburettor intake. The valve is operated by the carburettor heat control mounted on the instrument panel.

It would be very easy to misunderstand carburettor ice, its formation and the actions required to prevent and clear ice accretion. So it is important to understand the basic physics going on inside the throat of a carburettor venturi. Without getting too technical, as air passes through the venturi it speeds up, cools down and the local static air pressure decreases. The decrease in pressure provides the suction (fundamental to the function of a carburettor) to draw the fuel from the float chamber through the passages and into the airflow via the appropriate fuel jet. A jet is a very fine hole that regulates fuel flow. However, the downside of this process is that the cooling effects of the airflow is increased by the fuel evaporation, absorbing latent heat from the surroundings. So that the inside of a carburettor venturi can become very cold, freezing in fact, even though the outside temperature is quite warm. And if the humidity is high enough, we have a recipe for carburettor ice to form. As the venturi is already a fairly small place, it might not take long for enough ice to form, sufficient to restrict the venturi by an engine-stopping amount and turn your powered aircraft into a glider! Ice tends to build up on any protrusions or bends where the air contacts a surface at sub zero temperature and can occur on the ground as well as in flight.

We need to be on our guard for carburettor ice at any time, as it could really spoil your day if not spotted soon enough! One fallacy is to believe it needs to be cold or visible water present for ice to form in the carburettor. Obviously, to form ice, water is required and it is available in plentiful supply in vapour form in moist air masses; like those that usually cover most of the UK. Even in summer! Indeed warm air can support more water vapour than cold. As relative humidity is a measure of the water content of the air, this is a very useful guide as to how wet or dry the air is on a particular day. We know the temperature drop within the carburettor can be considerable (up to 30 degC) and water freezes at 0 degC and below. So, this combined knowledge helps us gauge the likely risk of carburettor icing on a given day. A very useful chart that elaborates on this phenomenon is produced by the CAA and is reproduced below. It can be seen that the ambient temperature does not have to be zero or 100% relative humidity for the risk of carburettor icing to be high. If not already familiar with the subject then further useful information can be found in AIC 145/1997 (Pink 161). As the ice forms in the carburettor it restricts the fuel air mixture rather like closing the throttle would. So, the first symptom in the C152 is a gradual loss of engine RPM. This may initially be overcome by an increase in the throttle setting, if not noticed as carburettor icing. Further icing would cause a further drop in engine rpm, leading to rough running and eventually engine failure. However, good engine management would encourage the pilot to operate the carb heat control on a regular basis. If ice is present in the carb, one of two reactions is likely on application of the carb heat. Either, the engine will start to cough a little as the ice is melted and water passes through the engine with an associated large drop in rpm. Or, the rpm will almost immediately start to increase. Neither of these being the normal response to checking the carb heat system, therefore warning the pilot of carb ice and that conditions are conducive to carb icing. With the foregoing in mind it is obvious that the carb heat control is an important engine management tool and why it should be checked carefully on the ground before flight. However, its use on the ground should be limited, because when selected it supplies the engine with an unfiltered source of air that could pass damaging airborne contaminants (dust, grit etc) which will increase engine wear. Also, using hot air to supply an engine operating at 75%hp or more is not recommended as detonation may occur, causing serious engine damage. Therefore always ensure that the carb heat is off when selecting full power. Using a source of hot air to run the engine also reduces the amount of power the engine can develop as it reduces its efficiency, as warm air is less dense than cold air.

The carb heat control should be thought of as a switch, either on (hot air) or off (cold air) and no in-between setting. To check its function, a note of the current rpm should be made, then select hot air (carb heat knob pulled out fully) for about 10 seconds. Note the small drop in rpm (50 –100) then reselect cold air (carb heat knob fully in). The rpm should return to the original value, if however it returns to a higher value then carb ice was present.

In the section discussing the mixture control we saw how it varied the fuel/air ratio, in selecting carb heat we also affect this ratio. The warm air supplied by the carb heat system, being less dense, causes an increase the richness of the mixture. Which for the temporary nature of a carb heat check is not a problem. However, if for some reason it was decided to fly with the hot air selected constantly on then the mixture control may have to be adjusted for best engine performance. During a descent when the carb heat is normally selected for the duration this is not an issue, as the mixture needs to be enriched anyway, and the overriding factor is the prevention of ice in the carb. It is also important that the carb heat is selected before reducing power to clear any ice prior to descent and check that it is still working correctly.

Extract from AIC 145/1997

3 Atmospheric Conditions

3.1 Carburettor icing is not confined to cold weather and will occur in weather if the humidity is high enough, especially when the throttle butterfly is only partially open as it is at low power settings. Flight tests have produced serious icing at descent power with the ambient (not surface) temperature above 30°C, even with a relative humidity as low as 30%. At cruise power, icing can occur at 20°C with a relative humidity of 60% or more. Ice accretion is less on cold, dry, winter days than on warm, humid, summer days because the water vapour content of the air is lower. Thus, where high relative humidity and ambient temperature of between -10° C and +25°C are common, as is the case in the UK and Europe, pilots must be constantly alert to the possibility of icing and should take the necessary steps to prevent it. If the appropriate preventive action has not been taken in time it is vital to be able to recognise the symptoms (see paragraph 4-2), so that corrective action can be taken before an irretrievable situation develops. Should the engine stop due to icing it may not re-start or, even if it does, the delay may result in a critical situation.

3.2 Carburettor or fuel icing may occur even in clear and these are, therefore, the most insidious of the various types of icing because of the lack of visual clues. The risk of all forms of induction system icing is higher in cloud than in clear air but because of the visual clues the pilot is less likely to be taken unawares.

3.3 Specific warnings of induction system icing are not included in standard weather forecasts for aviation. Pilots must use their knowledge and experience to estimate the likelihood of its occurrence from the weather information available. When information on the dewpoint is not available, pilots in the UK and Europe should always assume a high relative humidity, particularly when:

(a) The surface and low level visibility is poor, especially in the early morning and later evening and particularly when near large area of water;

(b) the ground is wet (even with dew) and the wind is light;

(c) just below the cloud base or between cloud banks or layers;

(d) in precipitation, especially if its persistent;

(e) in cloud or fog - these consist of water droplets and therefore the relative humidity should be to be 100%;

(f) in clear air where cloud or fog has just dispersed.

3-4 The chart below shows the wide range of ambient conditions conducive to the formation of induction system icing for a typical light aircraft piston engine. Particular note should be taken of the much greater risk of serious icing with descent power. The closer, the temperature and dewpoint readings the greater the relative humidity.

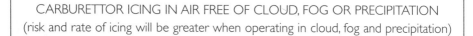

CARBURETTOR ICING IN AIR FREE OF CLOUD, FOG OR PRECIPITATION
(risk and rate of icing will be greater when operating in cloud, fog and precipitation)

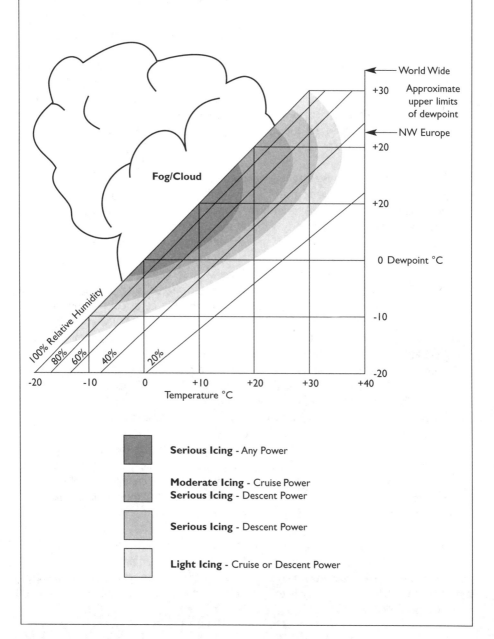

The Ignition System

The engine is fitted with a dual magneto ignition system. Two spark plugs being fitted in each cylinder and two magnetos mounted on the rear of the crankcase. High voltage capacity (also known as high tension) leads join the two components. There are two reasons for a dual ignition system. One, safety, should one system fail, secondly, due to the relatively large bore of the engine a better, more efficient fuel burn is achieved. The magnetos are termed left and right due to their respective positions on the engine. The magnetos are not connected to the rest of the electrical system and do not require any external electrical power source to function. A magneto uses the property of a moving magnetic field inducing an electric current in an adjacent coil of wire. In a magneto the magnetic field is rotated whenever the engine crankshaft is rotated, with the potential to generate a spark (at the spark plug) unless the primary (low voltage) circuit of the system is shorted out.

Due to the rotation of the magnetic field, an electric current is induced in the primary coils of the magneto which itself gives rise to another magnetic field around the coil so long as the circuit is complete. Also in the primary coil circuit is a set of contact breakers (that are controlled by the relative position of the crankshaft and magneto) and the mag switches. Considering only one cylinder, when the piston is at the correct position to receive a spark from the spark plug in order to fire, the contact breaker points open. This causes the magnetic field that has been created by the induced electric current in the primary coil to spontaneously collapse. With me so far, because it is a bit like the chicken and egg story! Additionally there is a secondary set of coils in the magneto assembly that have many more turns of wire than the primary coil. When the primary field collapses so spectacularly it induces a voltage in the secondary coil that by its nature will generate a voltage of many thousands of volts, enough to jump the gap in the electrodes of a spark plug. It is this voltage therefore that fires the mixture in the cylinder. This is then repeated for all the cylinders. The timing of the spark being crucial is controlled by a cam acting on the contact breaker. If the contact breaker is shorted out of the circuit then the primary coil magnetic field cannot collapse and no spark will be generated. This is what the magneto switches do. A glance at the wiring diagram below of a simplified typical magneto circuit shows the magneto switch in the on position which conventionally would be off, as in this condition it breaks the circuit. A reversal of what might be expected. Therefore, this shows the circuit in the live condition, to make it safe the magneto switch is closed which shorts out the action of the circuit breaker and therefore prevents a spark occurring at the spark plug.

Therefore the system is only safe when the primary circuit is short-circuited. So, if the switch fails or a wire becomes disconnected or broken then this would not be possible and the system would remain live. However, this has the advantage that it would not affect the ability of the engine to run. Hence, the respect and reason for always treating a propeller as live.

Simplified typical Magneto Wiring Diagram

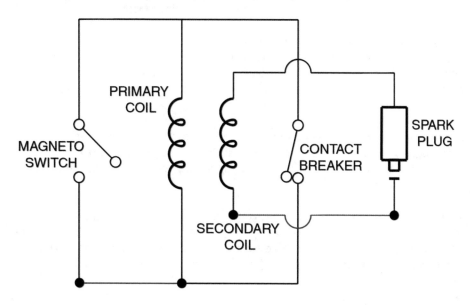

The blue link wires would normally be connections made through the frame of the aircraft called earthing, which reduces actual wiring.

The contact breaker remains in the closed position until opened by the action of crankshaft driven cam when a spark is required in one of the cylinders.

The Electrical System

Terminology used in this section that may require explanation.

Relay or Contactor: Electro-magnetic switch. A small wire coil is energised to produce a magnetic field capable of operating a switch very quickly with heavy electrical contacts. This enables a small electrical current to control an electrical circuit using a much larger current (e.g. a starter motor circuit). One advantage is the saving of weight by using shorter heavy cable runs.

Alternator: Electrical generating device capable of producing power even at low rpm. It produces alternating current that is passed through a rectifier/voltage regulator control unit converting it to direct current that can then be used in charging a battery and/or driving D. C. systems.

Bus: A common electrical rail which is connected to the circuit breakers.

Magneto: An assembly of fixed permanent magnets and wire coils on a spindle that when rotated generates a high voltage electrical current, used to power the spark plugs of an engine. Needs no external electrical power source to function.

Starter Motor: An electric motor requiring a very large current to produce sufficient torque to turn the engine over. It is only designed to operate for short intervals of time, otherwise it will overheat and burn out! When energised it engages automatically with a gear bolted to the crankshaft.

Circuit Breaker: An electrical device that will heat up when an electrical current in excess of the rated value is passed through it, causing a bimetal strip to open a pair of contacts, thus interrupting the current flow and consequently switching off the circuit. Generally these types of devices have replaced fuses in electrical circuits, as they are more convenient.

Power Supply

The Cessna 152 is fitted with a 28 Volt DC electrical system, powered by a 60 amp alternator. A 24 Volt battery is mounted on the right hand side of the engine bay. Fitted along side are the battery and starting contactors.

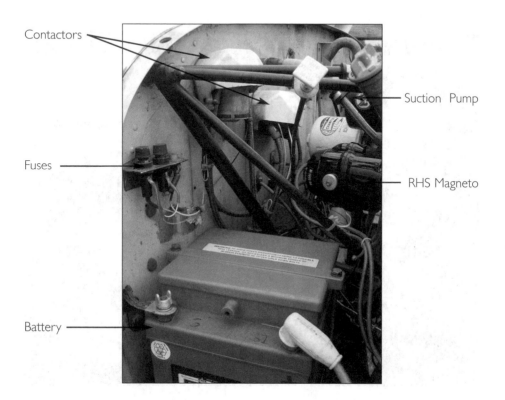

Contactors

Suction Pump

Fuses

RHS Magneto

Battery

The alternator is mounted on the front of the engine and driven through a V belt, (which should be checked before flight). Its electrical output being fed to a regulator unit mounted on the firewall before entering the rest of the system. The system is energised through the master switch, which is mounted on the lower left of the instrument panel. It is a dual-rocker type switch, which means the battery and alternator can be separately switched. Although normally it is operated as if it were a single switch. However the battery side could be used to check equipment on the ground before engine start. Beware though of the limited capacity of the battery, if overused it may not be possible to start the engine. A further point to note is that an alternator requires a small voltage before it will start supplying any electrical power, when rotated, called excitation. Therefore, if you have a flat battery and hand swing the prop to start the engine you may find that the alternator will not give any output. Some Cessna 152's are fitted with an external power supply socket. This is located on the left-hand side of the engine cowling. Before using this ensure the external power source is of the correct voltage (i.e. 24 Volts) and the master switch is on before connection. With the master switch on the engine can be started with the combined starter and magneto ignition switch.

If the electrical circuit diagram on page 38 is studied we can see that all electrical equipment is connected via circuit breakers to a common line or bus. Before the alternator is generating power the battery supplies all the electrical power to the bus through the ammeter. When the alternator is generating power it takes over the job of supplying power to the bus and also charges the battery. An ammeter is fitted into the circuit between the battery and the bus. This will then indicate whether power is flowing to or from the battery and what the level of current is. In normal circumstances it will show a small charge going to the battery after start to indicate a battery in good condition being topped up following the drain put on it by the starter motor. As well as an ammeter, a low voltage light is fitted to warn the pilot when the system voltage drops below normal. This may illuminate at low rpm and go out as the engine rpm increases, which is normal.

It may be tested by turning an electrical load such as the landing light on and momentarily turning off the alternator side of the master switch. The low voltage light should illuminate, then go out when the alternator is switched back on.

Power Consumption

It is a good idea to have some concept of the amount of electrical power the different systems on the aircraft consume. We can get an indication of this by the size of circuit breaker fitted to the circuit. Furthermore, if an item is not fitted with a switch it will be a very low consumer of power. For example the fuel gauges. At the other end of the scale, anything involving the generation of heat (such as a pitot heater) will be a large consumer of power. A motor (like that which drives the flaps) also requires a large current and the starter motor the most current of all. Lights come somewhere between the two extremes with, not surprisingly, the brighter the light the more power it requires. Therefore, if an alternator failure is suspected (this covered in more detail later) then the electrical load on the battery can be minimised by not using the high consumers especially, unless necessary.

Starting at bottom end of power consumption, the fuel gauges (one for each tank) are fitted to the lower left of the instrument panel and are powered by floating level sensors in the fuel tanks. As the float position varies with the amount of fuel so does the amount of power fed to the gauge. Beware that this is a very archaic system and very prone to inaccurate readings on the fuel gauges and any pre-flight check must include a visual check of the fuel tank contents. Compared the system and information displayed in a modern car it is quite prehistoric! However, the same could be said of all aircraft of similar vintage design. Adjacent to the fuel gauges are the oil temperature and pressure gauges. Of these two the temperature gauge is electrical receiving a signal from a sensor fitted into an oil gallery in the engine. The Turn Co-ordinator instrument fitted just above these gauges is also electrically operated and shares the same circuit breaker. Therefore, if you suspect the T/C is malfunctioning and the temperature gauge looks wrong, check the circuit breaker. Below these are all the main electrical switches. These are also rocker type switches and due to wear not always well labelled. Ensure that you are familiar with which switch operates what as there is some variation between aircraft models. The normal fit is to have navigation lights in each wing tip and tail, a rotating beacon, landing and taxi lights. Strobe lights may also be fitted in the wing tips.

Typical Switch Layout

As can be seen from the photo of a typical switch layout these mainly control the various lights fitted and the pitot heat. As mentioned before the pitot heat is a high consumer of power, which incidentally is at risk of burning out if left on too long whilst the aircraft is stationary on the ground. Adjacent to the rocker switches is a dual concentric rotating control for setting the interior light level. Labelled Panel Lt and Radio Lt. The Radio Lt knob is used to adjust the brightness of the radio stack illumination. The Panel Lt knob adjusts the brightness of either the overhead red 'flood' type lighting, or, if fitted, small post lights mounted next to each flight instrument. If post type lights are fitted, then a selector switch is also fitted in the overhead console for their control. A white light for cabin illumination is also fitted in the overhead console. A door post mounted map light may also be fitted. Obviously ensure that these are working before a night flight and which is the appropriate circuit breaker. As with the other circuit breakers it may be reset once if it has popped out, having allowed a short time for it to cool down.

Moving the flap switch lever down to one of the three stops actuates the electrically operated flaps. The lever needs to be moved slightly to the right and down to the first gate for 10 deg of flap. The same action is repeated for the 20 deg and 30 deg positions. Adjacent to the lever is a follow up indicator that displays the actual flap position. Visual confirmation that this display and operation is correct should be carried out on the ground before flight.

Starter Motor

A starter motor is fitted to the front lower left of the engine crankcase. The front end of which can be seen through the opening in the cowling. The ring gear that is bolted to the crankshaft can also be seen. When the starter key switch is operated, the starter motor rotates and the drive cog on the motor shaft is propelled along the shaft to engage with the ring gear, which then turns the engine. When the engine starts and the key released, power is disconnected from the starter motor and the drive cog should disengage and return to its original position. If it does not, then the engine will be rotating the starter motor. If this happens, as the engine rpm increases the starter motor could disintegrate in a rather alarming fashion! Also the motor will become a generator and could produce a potentially very damaging unregulated electrical power supply. Hence the reason for fitting a warning light for this condition. This is checked after start to show if the starter motor is still engaged.

Typical Simplified Starter Motor Circuit

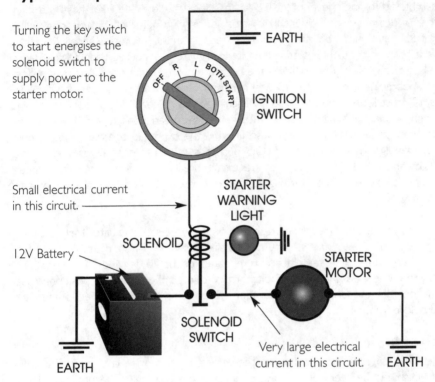

Turning the key switch to start energises the solenoid switch to supply power to the starter motor.

EARTH

IGNITION SWITCH

OFF R L BOTH START

Small electrical current in this circuit. →

STARTER WARNING LIGHT

SOLENOID

12V Battery

STARTER MOTOR

SOLENOID SWITCH

Very large electrical current in this circuit.

EARTH

EARTH

Avionics

The only remaining electrical consumers are the avionics or "Radio stack" which can vary enormously. Typically the aircraft will be fitted with a combined communication and navigation radio (nav/com) radio, a transponder and possibly an ADF receiver. Above the radio equipment an audio selector control panel is fitted and elsewhere on the instrument panel an intercom control panel. There are two types of Cessna audio control panel, one with marker beacon facility and one without. Both are used in much the same manner to select the relevant radio for headset or loudspeaker use. Although the marker beacon version seems to give the most confusion. A typical, although antiquated, radio stack is pictured below. At the top, the audio control panel (marker beacon version) can be seen. On the control panel the switch marked XMTR is a facility to switch between either of two com radios. However, normally a C152 would only be fitted with one such radio. To the right of this is a bank of switches that are used to select the aircraft loudspeaker or personal headset for audio output of the radios. If two radios are fitted then selecting COM AUTO (to speaker or headset) will automatically link the audio output of the receiver to the appropriate transmitter selected on the XMTR switch. Otherwise it would be possible to transmit on one frequency and be listening to the response on another, not very helpful! The COM BOTH switch is used to enable two stations to be monitored at one time, again either on the loudspeaker or headset. The remaining nav switches are used to select speaker or headset to listen out for audio transmissions on the particular nav radio selected. The radio stack picture shows a Cessna 300Nav/Com unit. This is a 720 channel VHF com receiver and 200 channel VHF navigation receiver. Most of the switches are self-explanatory, but the centre 5 – 0 switch sometimes proves to be a mystery to some operators. The main frequency selectors provide for switching in 0.050 mhz steps. For example from 123.450 mhz to 123.500 mhz To obtain a frequency of 123.475 mhz the 0-5 switch needs to be moved from position 0 to 5 (i.e. up). However, the display only allows for five digits to be displayed, so in this case we would see 123.47 mhz displayed.

A further example: With 0 selected 135. 90 dialled in, also = 135. 900
                                      With 5 selected 135. 90 dialled in, becomes 135. 925

One more click on the main frequency selector and returning the 0-5 switch to the 0 position would now give 135.95 and moving the 0-5 to the 5 position 135.975. Therefore, we can see that the 0-5 switch enables the operator to change the com radio frequency by 0.025 mhz steps giving the 720 channels between 118.00 mhz and 136. 00 mhz.

When identifying a navigation station the ID position needs to be selected on the VOX switch as well as the phone or speaker selector on the audio panel. The transponder is fairly standard with the usual four squawk code selectors and other facility buttons.

An ADF, if fitted as in the radio stack illustrated, also has a selector switch on the audio panel. Facilitating identification of the transmitter, as would a DME if fitted.

A radio stack looking remarkably similar in age to the aeroplane in which it is fitted!

Electrical System Malfunctions

The alternator is protected from electrical overload and over-voltage. Overload is controlled by the alternator circuit breaker. Over-voltage by an automatic control unit that monitors the system voltage and switches off the alternator should more than about 30 volts occur in the system. This helps to protect the voltage sensitive electronics in the rather expensive radios etc. If this were to occur, then the ammeter, mounted on the upper right side of the instrument panel, would show a minus reading. As the battery would be supplying all the electrical power. Depending on the electrical load at the time, the low voltage light will also illuminate. On early 152's an over-voltage light was also fitted, which would also illuminate to bring the condition to the attention of the pilot. However, it is possible that the condition was caused by a transitional peak in voltage and that the system would otherwise function correctly. It is possible to reset the automatic over-voltage unit by switching off the alternator side of the master switch for a couple of seconds and then back on again. If the reset has worked then the ammeter should show a normal reading and the low voltage light extinguish. If, however, the ammeter still shows a minus reading and the low voltage light is on, then the alternator has failed and a landing as soon as practicable should be considered. With the battery supplying all the electrical power it will last about 30 minutes with minimal load. It would be prudent to reduce the electrical load the minimum required for safe flight, remembering that the flaps are also electrically operated and are a high consumer, albeit for a short duration.

As explained before, the magneto system, which supplies the engine with electrical power to run, is completely separate from the normal electrical system. So any electrical system failure will not affect the ability of the engine to operate, allowing the pilot time to assess the probable cause. As we have seen, the individual systems are protected by circuit breakers that pop out if their load limit is exceeded. It is possible to try and reset these, but only once and only after a short period of time to allow them to cool down. Say a couple of minutes. However, if the tripped circuit breaker was accompanied by an acrid smell of burning plastic I would be rather suspicious that there was some form of short circuit that could lead to a fire and definitely not try to reset the breaker. But take some more immediate action to ventilate the cabin, identify the circuit concerned and its importance to the continuation of the flight. By cutting off the electrical power to the faulty circuit, the tripped circuit breaker has done its job, preventing the problem from getting worse. It is then up to the pilot to decide on the subsequent best course of action.

Electrical Circuit Diagram

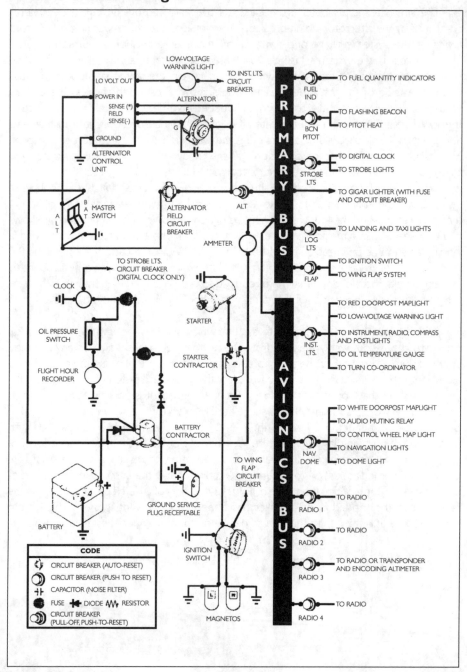

Vacuum System

The attitude and direction indicators are air-driven gyroscopic instruments, powered by the vacuum system. An engine driven vacuum pump provides a vacuum of 4. 5 to 5. 5 "hg below the ambient pressure and a gauge mounted on the instrument panel displays this. A relief valve/regulator is fitted to maintain the vacuum at the correct level and a reading outside the desired range implies a system malfunction. The pump is driven via a soft shearable drive coupling to prevent further problems should the pump seize. Should this occur the vacuum gauge reading would drop to zero. Air entering the system passes through an air filter to prevent damaging airborne particles reaching the instruments. If the filter does become clogged or blocked, a low reading would result as air enters the system through the regulator bypassing the instruments and gauge.

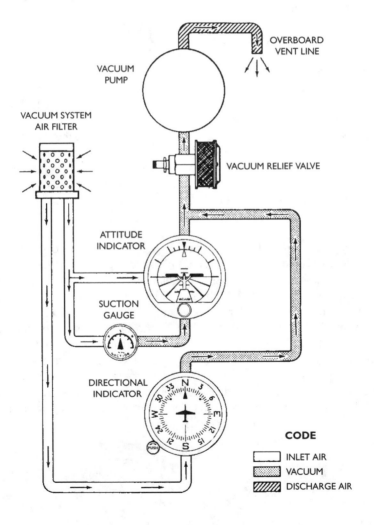

The Undercarriage and Brake System

The C150 was one of the first training aircraft to be fitted with tricycle under carriage and this was naturally carried forward onto the C152. Compared with tail wheel type aircraft it makes the take-off, landing and general ground handling much easier. Of course some "old bold pilots" looked down their noses at the idea of making learning to fly easier and still don't consider the C152 as a "real" aeroplane. However a pilots' flying skill should always be following a path of continuous improvement. Learning from others and by experience. With this in mind it makes sense to start with the simple and progress to the more difficult. So, in the C152 we have a very robust spring steel main undercarriage, which can, and do, absorb quite heavy impact with mother earth! The nose-leg however, is not so strong. As can be witnessed by the plethora of nose-leg collapse type accidents that adorn the accident reports.

For example: **From an AAIB report.**

Aircraft Cessna 152

The pilot was landing on runway 03 at XXXX, which had a published landing distanced of 871 metres. Its asphalt surface was dry and the PAPIs, set to 3.5 deg, were serviceable. The reported surface wind was 350/10kt with good visibility and no significant weather. The pilot reported that he was established on the runway centre line and glide path and at the correct speed. On touchdown however the aircraft bounced. The pilot briefly applied full power and then attempted a further landing during which the nose wheel collapsed and the propeller struck the runway surface. The pilot and his passenger, who were wearing lap and diagonal seat belts, vacated the aircraft without injury.

Something went wrong for which the aircraft was not designed and this wasn't a training incident, which are more prevalent. An oil and pressurised air oleo provides the shock absorbing qualities of the nose-leg. The unit is fitted to the engine frame that in turn is bolted to the firewall bulkhead. Although this is good at absorbing the shocks from undulations in ground whilst taxiing, a heavy landing on the nose wheel is a completely different matter. This would completely compress the oleo and pass the impact shock to the engine mounting. Deformation can then easily occur in the oleo itself and/or the engine mounting and possibly the bulkhead. And for good measure the propeller will probably chew up the runway. Not the desired outcome of a nice flight! It is therefore imperative that the initial landing load be absorbed by the main wheels that were designed to take it. The main wheels are fitted with independent single-piston hydraulic disc brakes.

Brake Disc

Caliper

Applying pressure to the tops of the rudder pedals operates the brakes. In doing so, the master cylinder fitted to each of the pedals mounted on the left-hand side of the aircraft (i.e. the pilots) forces brake fluid down the connecting pipes to the relevant wheel. The master cylinders are combined with a reservoir in one unit fitted to the pedals. A mechanical linkage is fitted so that the brakes can be operated from the rudder pedals on the right-hand side of the cockpit. To assist in manoeuvring the aircraft whilst taxiing differential brake pressure may be applied to either the left or right wheels as each system is totally independent. This makes the C152 very manoeuvrable, although as there is no rigid link between the nose wheel and rudder pedals, some practice is needed to master it completely. Care is also needed not to lock one wheel completely when turning tightly; otherwise excessive tyre wear will occur. The parking brake on the C152 is often misunderstood, although the system is very simple. It is also prone to malfunction, more often due to pilot misuse or abuse.

Main Wheel and Brake Assembly

Returning to the nose leg of the undercarriage, the oleo should be checked for the correct extension of about 75 mm. This ensures it can exhibit its required shock absorbing qualities. A trailing torque link is fitted to maintain correct wheel alignment, and a damper unit to reduce the effects of wheel shimmy whilst moving at high speed on the ground. The nose wheel is not rigidly linked to the rudder pedals for steering, but through a spring system. This at first seems vague and sloppy but with careful use of the differential brakes it is very effective, as the nose wheel will castor through up to 30 deg either side of straight ahead.

Park Brake Operating Knob

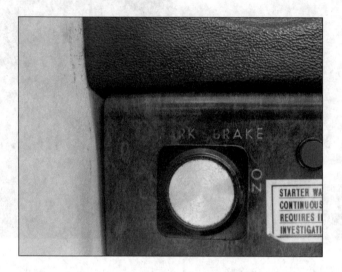

To operate the park brake correctly, firstly apply moderate pressure to toe brakes, whilst maintaining this pressure pull out the park brake knob. Then release the toe brake pressure and finally release the park brake knob, which should return to its original position. Due to nature of the system, the effectiveness of the park brake should be checked after vacating the aircraft by gently pushing on the wing strut to see if the aircraft moves. When applying the park brake be careful not to apply more pressure on the pedals than is necessary, as this can make it difficult to release them. To release the park brake, simply reapply pressure momentarily to the toe brakes and the park lock will come off. If it is found that park brake has not released on either one or both brakes by applying pressure to the pedals, then it can be done by hand but not whilst still sitting in the aircraft! Before describing how this is done it would be useful to understand how the brakes, and park brake in particular, actually work in the first place. With reference to the diagram opposite.

Brake Master Cylinders

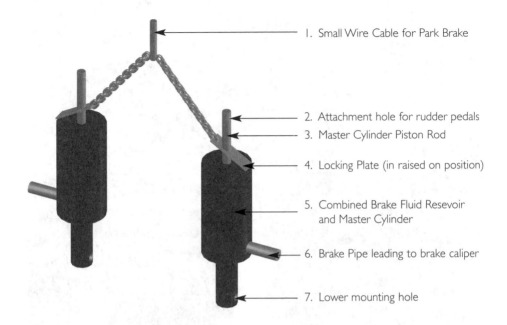

1. Small Wire Cable for Park Brake

2. Attachment hole for rudder pedals
3. Master Cylinder Piston Rod

4. Locking Plate (in raised on position)

5. Combined Brake Fluid Resevoir and Master Cylinder

6. Brake Pipe leading to brake caliper

7. Lower mounting hole

Applying pressure to the tops of the rudder pedals moves the master cylinder rod (2) downwards, which pushes fluid out through the brake pipe to pressurise the brake calliper on the appropriate wheel. This in turn causes the brake pads to grip the brake disc and hence slow down the wheel. To engage the park brake pressure is again applied, moving the rod (2) downwards. However, this time the pulling out the park brake knob, connected to cable (1), lifts the two locking plates (2), which simply yet effectively jamb the rod (2) in place. Thus maintaining pressure in the brake system even when the foot pressure is released, which ensures the pads continue to grip the disc and prevent wheel rotation. When, subsequently, foot pressure is applied to the pedals, the locking plates drop down the rod to rest on top of the master cylinder (5). So, returning to our original problem of releasing the park brake by hand if proving impossible by foot pressure. Assuming that the engine has been started, first of all shut it down, then from a standing position outside the aircraft, lean inside and release the locking plates by hand by pushing them down. This should only be necessary in extreme cases when someone has been a bit more than enthusiastic in applying the park brake!

Nose Wheel Assembly

Pitot Static System

The altimeter, airspeed indicator and vertical speed indicator are all connected to the pitot static system. The pitot head mounted under the left wing supplies the pitot pressure piot pressure for the airspeed indicator.

The static vent is mounted on the left side of the aircraft just in front of the door.

The pitot head is fitted with an electric heater element that is used to prevent blockage from ice. Remembering the proviso that the 152 is not cleared for flight in known icing conditions. However, it may inadvertently occur so ensure that it is working on the ground before flight. The vents themselves should be carefully checked. All sorts of bugs adore small holes to lay eggs and nest in, which would block the free passage of air and hence cause the instruments to malfunction. If something is found blocking a vent, then an engineer will probably be required to dismantle the vent to completely remove the offending article. Do not blow into the vent in order to dislodge the blockage, as this would probably make matters worse and may well damage the instruments.

Stall Warner Vent

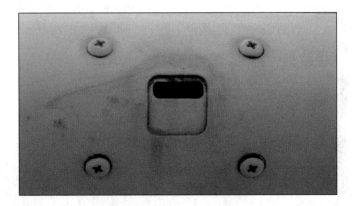

An audible stall warning device is fitted to alert the pilot to an impending stall. The approach to the stall is detected at the leading edge of the wing due to the change in airflow as the angle of attack nears the stall angle. As this happens a localised pressure depression occurs along the wing leading edge that coincides with the position of the stall warner vent. This causes air to be sucked through the vent. On the inside of the wing is a tube leading to the upper left fresh air vent in the cabin. Inside of the air vent a simple wind reed is fitted to the end of the tube. So when air is sucked through the tube via the stall warner vent it produces a musical note inside the cabin, thus warning the pilot that the aircraft is approaching the stall. The warning is typically about 5 – 10 kts above the stall. The closer the aircraft is to the stall the louder and higher pitch the warning note will be. The serviceability of the system can be checked on the ground by placing your mouth over the vent and sucking air through the system. However, it would be an extremely good idea to place a suitable cloth over the vent while you do this to prevent any unpleasant surprises coming from the vent! Also, the leading edges of wings are not usually the most cleanest of places so I would be prepared with a clean handkerchief.

Compass

The compass is mounted centrally near the top of the windscreen.

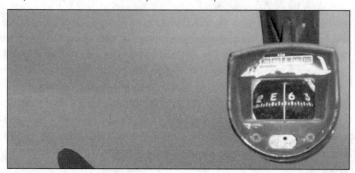

Outside air temperature gauge. This is fitted into the upper right fresh air vent.

Normal Operating Procedures

Preamble

The C152 is a very easy and forgiving aeroplane to fly. Which makes it an ideal abinitio trainer. Very little in its normal operating procedures should give the student, or qualified pilot alike, cause for concern. Although the C152 has few vices, like all aircraft, if operated incorrectly it is quite capable of, as a minimum, embarrassing the pilot. One problem that would quickly become apparent to a low wing pilot is that of visibility during turning, the lower wing blanking the view into the turn. However, this is balanced by the better view below when navigating or just sight seeing. Although some tips and advice on handling is given this section nothing, however, should override the guidance given by a flying instructor familiar with the type, but rather as reinforcement and addition to knowledge given during flying training.

Safe on the ground

The common practice of parking light aircraft pointing into wind applies particularly to the C152 due to the high wing design. It is more affected by strong and gusty winds than a low wing type and more lightly to be flipped over on to its back if not parked and tied down correctly. If a C152 is likely to be exposed to such winds then it should be tied down using the tie down points fitted to the top end of each wing strut. The tie down point under the tail should also be used if the wind direction is expected to change to blow from behind the aircraft, or if the aircraft is going to unattended for some time. I once saw a Cessna that had been tied down using the strut points quite correctly but a few days later with a strong tail wind flipped over forwards still attached to its tie downs! Another precaution, against wind damage, possible when the aircraft is parked on grass, is to dig out a small trough for the nose wheel to sit in which reduces the lifting power of the wings when wind blows over them. The C152 is provided with a control lock for the yoke that protects to the ailerons and elevator from wind damage and should always be fitted when parked.

Also the pitot tube should be covered when the aircraft is parked to prevent the ingress of bugs and other airborne contamination that could affect the function of the airspeed indicator due to a blockage of the tube. The parking brake should also be applied, although the C152 is a rather "Heath Robinson" affair, as described in the brake section. After exiting the aircraft following brake application it is worth checking that the park brake is effective by trying to gently push on the wing strut to test for movement. If the park brake proves to be ineffective then chocks should be placed around the wheels.

Starting

Starting the C152 is fairly straightforward. With the master switch on, open the throttle about ¼" – ½" (5-10 mm) prime the engine using 3 – 4 strokes and then turn the magneto key switch until the starter engages and turns the engine. After starting the engine rpm should be adjusted to about 1200 rpm. If the engine does not start after, say, 10 – 15 seconds of cranking then it is probable that the engine is either under or over primed. It is better to stop cranking the engine and decide on a further course of action than continue. If during the attempt to start the engine it fired erratically and puffs of black smoke were seen to come from the exhaust. Then a flooded or over primed engine is the likely cause. If this is the case, then fully open the throttle and select ICO on the mixture control then operate the starter again. As the engine starts retard the throttle and move the mixture to the fully rich position. This is best done with three hands! Alternatively leave starting for 10 – 15 minutes to allow the fuel to evaporate. If, however, during start the engine does not fire at all then it is probably under primed for the conditions (i. e. cold) and further priming will be required. Do not try "pumping" the throttle as this can cause an excess of fuel to collect in the carburettor with the attendant fire risk on models fitted with an accelerator pump. Also, the engine does not "suck in" the fuel provided by the primer so well with the throttle wide open, which applies to models with or without an accelerator pump. The aircraft is fitted with a warning light that illuminates when the starter motor is operated. If it remains on after starting the engine, damage to the starter motor and electrical system could occur and so the engine should be immediately shut down. Assuming this is not the case, then the oil pressure gauge should be checked next, to ensure that the oil pressure is rising within 30 seconds to within the green arc. Again if this is not apparent then shut down the engine before serious damage is caused. Other system gauges should also be checked at this point such as suction and ammeter gauges, followed by other checks set out in the "After start check list".

Taxying

The C152 is very manoeuvrable on the ground although some practice may be needed to fully utilise this ability. Due to the fact that the nose wheel is linked to the rudder pedals by a spring link system, the steering seems less positive than on aircraft with direct linkage. The rudder pedal linkage actually only moves the nose wheel through about 10° either side of centre and use of differential braking is required to increase this up to the maximum of 30°. This enables the C152 to be manoeuvred in very small spaces quite accurately, although caution is needed to prevent total lock-up of a wheel, which can cause tyre scrubbing. As a result of having a semi-castoring nose wheel, rudder will be required to prevent weathercocking when taxying in a crosswind. This is also a reason for using care when applying the brakes to slow down during taxying. When reducing speed the throttle should be closed first, but following this it should be reset to 1000 – 1200 rpm to help prevent spark plug fouling. The speed used for taxying depends on the surface being traversed. When crossing a grass surface particular care needs to be taken to avoid potential damage being caused by travelling too fast over a surface that may be rutted, uneven or have soft patches. It is also normal practice to test the brake function shortly after commencing taxying, although a brake pressure test could be carried out before moving off.

The diagram below shows the recommended positions for the control column depending on the prevailing wind conditions.

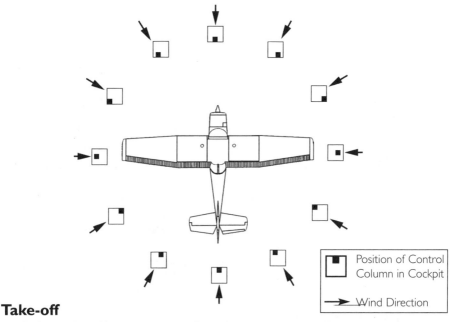

Take-off

Before take-off, a normal set of power and pre take-off checks is carried out. Normally the aircraft is positioned into wind to carry out these checks, which aids engine cooling. Also, the controls will be buffeted about if the wind is blowing from behind the aircraft whilst the checks are completed. With the aircraft in the correct place, normally the engine is opened up to 1700rpm and the carb heat checked first, with a drop of approx 50rpm being a typical and correct result. It should be remembered, that as explained in the engine section the carb heat supplies the engine with an unfiltered source of air and should therefore be used only as and when necessary. Otherwise dust and other airborne particles will pass into the engine, which would lead to increased wear. Following the carb heat the magnetos are checked individually. The maximum permissible drop is 125rpm with difference between the two of no more than 50rpm. Although a lower rpm is witnessed when operating on one magneto the engine should still run smoothly and if not then a fouled spark plug may be the problem. It is sometimes possible to clear a fouled plug by increasing the rpm to about 2000 (with magnetos on both) and leaning off the mixture to give the maximum rpm for a short time.

Then return the mixture to the rich position and recheck the magnetos. If the problem has disappeared it is fine to carry on, if not then the aircraft requires the attention of an engineer as problem may be more serious. Following a successful magneto check oil pressure and temperature, suction and ammeter indications are checked at 1700 rpm too. The throttle is then closed to check the idling rpm is between 500-700 and that oil pressure and ammeter readings are within limits. Following this the pre take-off checks are carried out from the check list to ensure the aircraft is correctly set up for take-off, then review the wind direction for crosswind component and its potential affect. The maximum demonstrated crosswind is 12 kts although each pilot should recognise his own limits and currency. It is important to be able to quickly and mentally calculate the approximate crosswind from a given wind velocity. One method (and there are several) is to use the face of a watch to aid the calculation. The diagram below may help to see how this is done. First of all, work out the angular difference between the runway direction and the wind direction. Then, looking at our watch face imagine the 15 minute position to represent 15 deg., 30 minutes /30 deg, 45 minutes/45 deg, 60 minutes/60 deg. These increments also represent $1/4$, $1/2$, $3/4$ and a full watch face respectively. We then return to the wind velocity given, use the angular difference between the wind and runway to arrive at the fraction of a watch face and multiply the wind speed by this fraction. E. g. wind 30 deg off the runway at 18 kts. 30 deg = 30 min = $1/2$ a watch face, therefore $1/2 \times 18 = 9$ kts of crosswind. A quick and simple method to work out the crosswind component. Anything more than 60 deg would be treated as all crosswind. Although not mathematically pure, it is good enough and easy to apply even when on final approach to land or just prior to take off.

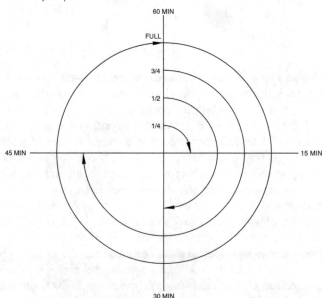

WIND 30 DEG FROM R/W DIRECTION IS READ AS 30 MINUTES ON
OUR WATCH FACE AND THEREFORE HALF THE WIND SPEED

Following the line up on the runway ensure heels are on the floor to prevent inadvertent brake application and smoothly increase the power to full. As a guide the throttle should be opened from normal idle (1200 rpm) to full power over a count of about 4. This avoids too rapid an increase in power, which is not good for the engine or directional control of the aircraft. Once the aircraft is directionally stable then a check to see that full power is being developed, about 2350 rpm at this stage and that oil pressure and temperature are normal. Also check that the airspeed is increasing.

For a normal take–off the nose wheel is lifted off the runway at about 50 kts and climb away at 65 kts/70 kts. If a short field performance takeoff is required, then 10 deg of flap is used and an initial climb speed of 54 kts to give best angle of climb. After the initial climb of say 200/300 ft the airspeed should be increased and the flaps retracted once 60 kts is achieved. Significant variations in stated aircraft performance can result by operating from airfields with a surface other than paved, high temperature or high altitude and due allowances should be made. This is covered further in the performance section. Also, extra care should be taken when taking off from a rough grass surface to protect the propeller, by the application of a bit more back pressure on the control column during the roll.

After the initial climb, if no obstacles remain to be cleared, it is better to adopt more of a cruise climb at 70 to 80 kts. This gives better engine cooling and an improved view ahead. However, it is still important to monitor the engine oil temp. and pressure, and weave or lower the nose to see clearly ahead of the aircraft. At higher altitudes in the climb (above 5000) it will be necessary to lean the mixture to obtain max power from the engine.

Cruising

With reference to the performance tables it can be seen that there can be significant differences in fuel consumption depending upon what power setting is used and altitude flown. Typically 55% to 65% power would be used, this gives reasonable fuel consumption and 85 to 95 kts of airspeed. The choice is yours! But an important planning issue is the endurance expected and the endurance achieved, which not only lies with the power and altitude selected but correct use of the mixture control. As we observed earlier in the section referring to the leaning procedure. More of this topic is discussed in the performance section on cruise performance. During any flight it is of the up-most importance to maintain good engine management throughout, as accidents as a result of poor fuel management or carburettor ice detection still feature highly in AAIB reports. As mentioned earlier the fuel gauges are not highly accurate and any pre-flight check should include a visual check and careful calculation of the amount of fuel on board. Then ensure that it is enough for the flight, taxying, take-off, landing, diversion if necessary and some in reserve. Also, one should bear in mind that try as we might to achieve the book performance figures, we probably won't; as our aircraft is unlikely to be in the same mint condition as the one used to produce the figures and we are also unlike to have the skill of the test pilot! Of course, fuel and carburettor ice are not the only engine factors to consider. The general health of the engine is displayed on the oil temperature and pressure gauges, and audibly by the way it sounds. An immense silence from up front tells you an awful lot about the health of the engine! However, by careful monitoring we may spot an impending problem before it gets to that stage. When oil is cold it is a quite viscous fluid like condensed milk! But as it gets hot it thins out to be more like normal milk! And the hotter it gets the thinner or more watery it gets. Inside an engine one of the most important tasks an oil has to perform is that of lubrication. To do this, as we saw before, it is pumped around the engine by the oil pump to those parts requiring it. Having lubricated the relevant parts it leaks out back to the sump. The problem we have, is that the thinner the oil the easier it is for it to leak back to the sump before performing the lubrication; and also to leak internally around the pump, preventing it from producing the correct pressure in the first place. So. if we observe a high oil temperature reading combined with a low oil pressure our engine is likely to very shortly be in the initial throws of self-destruction followed by that immense silence!

Therefore, some immediate action is called for. It maybe that it is a particularly hot day and you have just got to the top if a long slow climb without observing the gauges in the climb. Lowering the nose attitude and reducing power to the cruise may restore things to normal. However, serious consideration should be given to the idea of terminating the flight as soon as possible. If, however, there is an erroneous reading on one gauge only then it may just be a faulty gauge or sensor, but in any case the pilots best course of action would probably be to divert to the nearest airfield for further inspection. During the cruise monitoring of other system gauges like the suction and ammeter should also of course be carried out to warn the pilot of problems in those areas. Having a high mounted wing embodies the C152 with a good characteristic for navigation and stability. Combined with light controls and excellent trimmer makes it a delight to fly. In all normal and abnormal (stalling, spinning) manoeuvres it performs without vice.

Stalling

A stall in the C152 is conventional and quite docile. There is very little buffet in the clean, power off, stall and if held in the stall during training this can be demonstrated. Recovery, using a standard stall recovery technique with power would typically require about 100 –150 ft once initiated. The stalling speed in this condition varies a bit with the position of the centre of gravity but would be around 36-40 kts. The flight manual lists the stall speeds with a forward and rearward C of G and various flap settings, all of which will vary the actual stall speed. Although, at these low airspeeds and high angle of attack the airspeed indicator suffers significantly from position error, causing it to under read. The speed at which the stall warner sounds, in relation to the actual stall, can be adjusted, but is typically about 5-10 kts above the stall.

Stalling with power and flap is likely to induce a wing drop at the stall unless the aircraft is kept in balance, which would reduce this tendency. However, dealt with correctly under the guidance of an instructor this should not prove too difficult to master.

Spinning

The C152 can be a reluctant spinner. Usually, you have to work at it to get the aircraft into a spin, unless you are doing something aerobatic already. And, although not the recommended method, if you were to simply let go of the controls it would probably come out of the spin of its own accord, albeit in a rather low nose attitude. I repeat, probably and not recommended! Entry into a spin to the left is easiest, and will usually require about 1500 rpm. Applying full left rudder and full up elevator at around 50-55 kts normally does the job. Initially an incipient spin is entered followed a tightening up into the full spin in what might appear to be a vertical attitude!

Often quite alarming to the unsuspecting first timer. However, recovery is quite straightforward and once again, needs to be learn from an instructor at a safe altitude. Essentially, the recovery would involve ensuring the throttle is closed, flaps are up, identify the direction of spin and apply full rudder in the opposite direction. As the rudder hits the stop move the control column centrally forward until the spin stops, when it does - centralise the rudder and ease out of the ensuing dive! Normally in the C152 as soon as you start the recovery procedure the spin will stop, and it will all be over before you know it. This is because it is a very low nose attitude spin and therefore not very stable. If the spin were flatter (i. e. nose attitude higher) it would be more stable and therefore take longer to recover. However these are slight generalisations and there is no substitute for proper training. Do-it-yourself aerobatic training is about as clever as do-it-yourself brain surgery!

Approach and Landing

During a descent is another time to remind ourselves that power plus attitude equals performance. The aircraft can descend with power varied from idle (glide descent) to around 2000 rpm (cruise descent). Which you choose to use depends upon the circumstances. For a given airspeed, the greater the reduction in power, the greater the rate of descent. When using power settings of less than 2000 rpm it is usual to select full carb heat first to prevent carb icing occurring, reselecting cold air if full power is required for a "Go Around". Lowering flaps will also increase the rate of descent. Normally deployed during the initial stages of approach, lowering flap causes the nose to initially pitch up which should be prevented followed by a reduction in airspeed. Usually 20 deg of flap would be selected on base leg of a circuit and 30 deg on final approach. This is a very important time to ensure that the aircraft is correctly trimmed as there is significant trim change when flaps are deployed and it is highly likely that the aircraft will be flying at a low airspeed.

Throughout the descent a scan should be maintained to ensure that the aircraft is doing what we intended in terms of performance and correcting for any errors. This can be usefully practised at altitude away from the pressure of a landing.

There can be few aircraft easier to land than a C152, but it can quickly go very wrong if the approach is not flown correctly. Of course the second part of that statement applies to any aircraft, although the Cessna is quite forgiving. As with any aircraft, the trick is for the pilot to be ahead of the aircraft. Like any sport, anticipation is the name of the game. The question on our mind should always be, what is it going to do next? A similar thought process used when playing a game of, say, tennis or squash. If this is considered then the pilot can make a control input exactly when it is required. As there will always be a delay between control input and response of the aircraft. That said, in normal conditions if the approach is flown at the correct speed of around 65 kts reducing to 60 kts over the numbers, flaring at the appropriate height (which can only learnt by demonstration), closing the throttle and holding off until a touch down on the main wheels first is assured; then an acceptable landing is likely to be the result. Most problems arise from approaching at an inappropriate speed, the aircraft being aimed at the threshold or numbers with little regard for the aircraft speed or wind conditions. This is likely to result in "ballooning" at the flare or "bouncing" on touch down, both of which should elicit an immediate "Go Around". Of course there are many problems that can plague a pilot when learning to land, which can lead to a certain amount of frustration. However, analysis by a flying instructor and guidance in the correct techniques should ensure this is overcome effectively. Landing accidents due to mishandling in this critical phase of flight are quite common, as mentioned earlier, although quite avoidable. Firstly, by using the correct technique to land and secondly, to have the presence of mind, airmanship, to "Go Around" if it starts to go wrong. Remember, anticipation, if you wait until it has gone wrong it's probably too late and you will need some assistance to retrieve the propeller and nose leg from the runway!

If a short field approach is required then the threshold speed should be 54 kts with full flap, but beware of getting too slow on the final approach. At this speed the hold off will be of shorter duration. The brakes would then be firmly applied after landing. If a "Go Around" is carried out from this approach, consideration must be given to the low speed and full flap configuration when initiating the procedure. Preventing the nose attitude rising too far when full power is applied will require considerable forward pressure on the control column. Raising the 30 deg stage of flap at the first opportunity is also a must, to improve the climb performance. But this could also be the case if going around from the latter stages of a normal landing.

Should the flaps fail, a flapless landing would be approached with a slightly higher airspeed of 65 – 70 kts. In this case the hold off would be much longer with a much less pronounced flare and therefore requiring a much longer landing distance.

After touchdown on the main wheels the back pressure on the control column, required for the correct landing attitude, is gradually relaxed allowing the nose wheel to gently come into contact with the runway. With the good directional control that the cessna possesses it is relatively easy to keep straight during the roll out.

Performance

Preamble and terminology used in this section

An aircraft's performance will vary greatly depending upon a number of factors. A performance table will normally give the pilot the basic raw data for say, a take-off distance. This figure however may not take into consideration the difference in aircraft performance that maybe achieved in conditions that differ vastly from those of the test aircraft. Any variation in those conditions should be assessed for, and their effect on the aircraft's subsequent performance and the difference calculated. This process is called factoring. The CAA in AIC 67/2002 (Pink 36) gives guidance information on light aircraft performance, which can also be found in a safety sense leaflet currently published in the back of LASORS. I strongly recommend this as further reading on the subject, if you are not already familiar with the document. It sets forth general information on the subject and also correction factors that are recommended for use when adjusting raw data performance figures for actual conditions. Also, in our case, Cessna produce the information within the performance section of the P. O. H. to cope with many circumstances. How the pilot loads and handles the aircraft and manages the engine will also affect the performance achieved. In the next section we will deal with how to correctly load the C152 and the loading limits. The flight manual section on performance assumes that the aircraft is loaded to its maximum take-off weight and that this weight is correctly distributed to maintain the centre of gravity within the prescribed limits. The tables and graphs in the performance section are used by the pilot to obtain the information necessary to achieve a particular performance, be it climb, cruise or descent etc. However, it would be wise to remember that the information provided within this section would have been achieved by a very experienced test pilot in a brand new aircraft! If you and your aircraft are not in the same category then additional allowances need to be made for safety, especially in the take-off and landing phases. For this reason it would be prudent to 'factor', or multiply any take-off or landing performance figure, obtained from the tables, by the recommended public transport safety factors. These being 1.33 and 1.43 respectively. There may be other reasons for further factoring such as surface condition or temperature, as we shall see later. Although samples tables are reproduced in this booklet, to demonstrate their use, always ensure that you use the data from the actual flight manual of the aircraft being used for operational purposes. As there may well be a C. A. A. amendment sheet for certain performance criteria inserted into the flight manual/P. O. H. Each table or graph in the P. O. H. will be accompanied by a list of conditions that applied to the aircraft when that data was produced. So, any variation from these conditions needs to be considered and if necessary adjusted for, or 'factored'.

At the end of the day we must ensure that any distances (be it take off or landing) that our aircraft requires is less than that which is available, otherwise we are asking for trouble.

(Illustrations of TORA, TODA and LDA LRA)

TORR   Takeoff run required. Runway length required to become airborne.

TODR   Takeoff distance required. Distance required to become airborne and clear an imaginary barrier 50 ft high.

LRR   Landing run required. Runway length required from touch down to achieving a full stop.

LDR   Landing distance required. Distance required to touch down after clearing an imaginary 50 ft barrier plus the landing run required.

TORA   Take off run available.

TODA   Take off distance available.

LRA   Landing run available.

LDA   Landing distance available

Pressure Altitude:

For airfield elevation purposes this equates to the altitude displayed on the altimeter with the aircraft on the ground and the sub-scale set to the standard setting of 1013 mb.

With reference to the extract from AIC 67/2002 shown below we can see the sort of factors that will affect an aircraft's performance and how we can adjust for them. However, this is probably best illustrated by working through an example as shown below.

AIC 67/2002

Para 1. 3   Aeroplane Performance is subject to many variables including:

Aeroplane weight
Aerodrome altitude
Temperature
Wind
Runway length, slope and surface
Flap setting
Humidity

Para 5. 8   Humidity

High humidity has an adverse affect on performance and this is usually taken into account during certification, however, there may be a correction factor applicable to your aeroplane. Consult the manual. Apart from the humidity issue, the above variables can be factored for and flap setting is given as a condition of the performance table.

Take-off Performance

It can be seen from the performance table extract below, that the table in the C152 P. O. H. allows the pilot to obtain a take-off distance or ground roll factored directly for altitude and temperature. This figure is then adjusted as required depending upon the conditions.

Let us assume we are going to visit an unfamiliar airfield, Landaway Farm, for the first time! We have been diligent enough to obtain the airfield information and conditions needed to carry out our calculations. Then, as take-off distances are generally more than landing we are firstly going to check that we will be able to get airborne following a successful arrival.

Conditions at Landaway Farm are:

Runway length 850 m
Short dry grass runway
Wind calm
Airfield elevation 390 ft
Temperature +25°C
QNH 993 mb

Firstly, we study the performance table extract and work out a basic take-off distance and ground roll figure for the relevant temperature and altitude. If, as in our case, there is not a figure that directly relates to the particular temperature or altitude then we can either pick next higher figure or interpolate between the two nearest. The first method builds in a bit more safety and the second takes more time but is more accurate. Bearing in mind at all times your own level of skill the choice is yours. We will work both out.

Take off performance table extract:

WEIGHT LBS	TAKEOFF SPEED KIAS LIFT OFF	TAKEOFF SPEED KIAS AFT 50FT	PRESS ALT FT	0°C GRND ROLL	0°C TOTAL TO CLEAR 50FT OBS	10°C GRND ROLL	10°C TOTAL TO CLEAR 50FT OBS	20°C GRND ROLL	20°C TOTAL TO CLEAR 50FT OBS	30°C GRND ROLL	30°C TOTAL TO CLEAR 50FT OBS	40°C GRND ROLL	40°C TOTAL TO CLEAR 50FT OBS
1670	50	54	SL	640	1190	695	1290	755	1390	810	1495	875	1605
			1000	705	1310	765	1420	825	1530	890	1645	960	1770
			2000	775	1445	840	1565	910	1690	980	1820	1055	1960
			3000	855	1600	925	1730	1000	1870	1080	2020	1165	2185
			4000	940	1775	1020	1920	1100	2080	1190	2250	1285	2440
			5000	1040	1970	1125	2140	1215	2320	1315	2625	1420	2750
			6000	1145	2200	1245	2395	1345	2610	1455	2855	1570	3125
			7000	1270	2470	1375	2705	1490	2960	1615	3255	1745	3590
			8000	1405	2800	1525	3080	1655	3395	1795	3765	1940	4195

Firstly, we need to appreciate that the table shows pressure altitude and not just airfield elevation.

So, we can either set 1013 mb on the altimeter sub-scale and read off the pressure altitude, or calculate it. Using the approximate figure of 30ft per millibar.

As the airfield pressure is lower than standard, 1013, (on which the tables are based) then the resulting performance will be as if the airfield were 1013 – 993 (20 mb) higher than it actually is. We can then convert this 20mb to a height (30 × 20) of 600 ft Add to this its actual elevation of 390 ft and finally arrive at our pressure altitude of 990 ft!

Secondly, using the next highest value for temperature in the table (i.e. 30c) and 1000 ft pressure altitude we produce a figure of 890ft for the ground roll. And 1645 ft to clear a 50 ft obstacle or otherwise known as TODR. Having obtained this basic figure we can now apply any differences from the list of conditions listed in the POH above performance table. The conditions given in the POH are:

Use flight manual technique for a short field take-off
Airfield at sea level and pressure 1013mb
Paved, level, Dry runway
Zero wind

As the C152 table effectively factors for the temperature and altitude directly we now only need to factor for the grass and safety.

From the table below reproduced from AIC 67/2002 we can derive the factors or multipliers that we need to apply to our basic TODR to obtain the correct value for our particular set of conditions at Landaway Farm. Therefore, in our case, all we need to do is multiply the basic TODR by the factor for grass (1.2) and safety (1.33).

Basic TODR from table 1645

Factored TODR = 1645 x 1.2 x 1.33 = 2625 ft
A considerable difference!

To convert feet to metres multiply by 0. 3048.
2625 x 0.3048 = 800 m
Compare this TODR 800 m with the TODA at Landaway Farm

Obviously, if we had a TODR greater than TODA then we have a problem! Remember these factors are only recommendations, and it is up to you ,the pilot, to ensure that your aircraft has the correct potential performance to meet the requirements. Ignoring them if things look a bit tight is foolhardy and you do so at your peril. Consequently improving your chances of becoming another "through the hedge at the end of the runway statistic". Whether or not you are able to walk away from such an incident is a matter of luck and if you trust luck I suggest that you read a few more accident reports. I once heard that in aviation you start with a bag full of luck and an empty one of experience, unfortunately the bag of luck has a small hole in it, and the trick is to fill the one of experience before the one of luck runs out! I suggest that luck is not the best way to view safety.

Furthermore, if on this calm day a slight tailwind (of say 5 kts) were to pick up then this distance would become 3162 ft or 958 m!

Converting the distance to metres is required when to comparing UK runway distances that are published in metres. Therefore, with a runway length of 850 m it should be no problem as long as recommended take-off technique is used and 50 metres of runway is not used for lining up. Remember that runway behind you is as good as fuel in the bowser! Interpolating more exactly would reduce the initial figure from the table to 1588ft and the final figure to 772 m.

The takeoff run required or ground roll figure from the table would be 890 ft. Factoring this figure for grass and safety;

890 x 1.2 x 1.33 = 1420 ft or 433 m

However, if a take off distance available is not declared then use the runway length as the take off distance available and compare this with your take off distance required. As you will not know what obstacles may stand immediately off the end of the runway just waiting to spoil your day!

Take off Performance Factors

Condition	Increase in take off distance	Multiplication Factor
A 10% increase in aircraft weight	20%	1. 20
An increase of 1000ft in aerodrome altitude	10%	1. 10
An increase of 10∞C in ambient temperature	10%	1. 10
Dry grass * Up to 20cm (8") (on firm soil)	20%	1. 20
Wet grass * Up to 20cm (8") (on firm soil)	30%	1. 30
A 2% uphill slope*	10%	1. 10
A tailwind component of 10% of lift off speed	20%	1. 20
Soft ground or snow*	25% or more	1. 25+

*Effect on ground roll will be proportionately greater

So, from our calculations we now know that it is quite feasible to take off from our intended destination, what remains is to work out how much runway we need to land. Another pause for though though would be to consider how much runway you need to stop your beloved steed if you decide to abandon the take-off at nearly lift off speed? Some idea can be gleaned from the landing run table as you will be at a similar speed. Even more runway please!

Landing Performance

As we have seen the take-off distance an aircraft requires can vary considerably when it is operated in differing conditions. So too is the landing distance. Once again when planning a trip, in particular, to an unfamiliar airfield it would be very poor airmanship not to carry out a landing performance calculation. AIC 67/2002 also gives us guidance in how to adjust the landing distance required for the variables that will affect it. For convenience the table from that AIC is reproduced below. So, working through our example at Landaway Farm again, we will calculate our actual LDR and LRR.

Assume conditions as above and approach using short field technique.

Therefore:

Basic LDR from table 1270 ft

As in the case for take off, further factoring for the grass surface (1.15) and a recommended safety margin (1.43) is required with the information from the table below.

Factored LDR 1270 x 1.15 x 1.43 = 2088 ft
Converting to metres 2088 x 0.3048 = 637 m.

LRR 500 ft x 1.2 x 1.43 = 858 ft or 261 m

As the LDA is 850 m and our LDR is 637 m there should not be a problem. So long as we fly the aircraft in the correct manner so as to achieve the performance figures quoted. Therefore you might need to review the correct short field technique recommended in the flight manual. Approaching at 10 kts above the correct speed, with only partial flap and touching down well down the runway is a guaranteed recipe for unintentional hedge cutting in the shape of an aeroplane! I think they call it topiary, but best not done with a propeller! If the approach does not seem to be working out when you get there, may be its not your day, don't let any pressure force you to try and land. Go home and practice your short field technique on a long runway first, make up a spot landing competition for yourself, and only accept perfection! The runway I have used as an illustration is not particularly short and there are many that offer far more limiting distances, but with the right conditions and experience these offer interesting places to visit. Carrying out the performance calculations is only one half of the story, the other is you being able to fly the aeroplane in the correct manner so as to achieve the performance. Only you can answer that and do not be too proud to ask an instructor for a lesson on how to achieve the outcome you desire. They are not there just for basic training, but also to help you develop you piloting skills as you acquire more experience, remember we are all, always learning. This reminds me to mention that with all the forgoing completed and assessed we have not even mentioned the effect of a crosswind on the proceedings or that of a gusty day. This should also be considered. Is it a narrow runway or slightly scaled down Heathrow? In my capacity as a Flight Instructor Course instructor I am frequently presented with pilots holding a commercial licence who can't land for toffee in a crosswind. We definitely just arrive! And, as we have to operate off a fairly narrow runway it is a rather important skill that may not be required so much at a larger aerodrome. But operating into or out of a smaller runway it takes on a more important significance. This is another skill that can easily be improved and result in an immense feeling of satisfaction, conquering a sometimes mystifying talent.

Landing Performance Factors

Condition	Increase in landing distance	Multiplication Factor
A 10% increase in aircraft weight	10%	1. 10
An increase of 1000 ft in aerodrome altitude	5%	1. 05
An increase of 10°C in ambient temperature	5%	1. 05
A wet paved runway	15%	1. 15
Dry grass * Up to 20 cm (8") (on firm soil)	15%	1. 15
Wet grass * Up to 20 cm (8") (on firm soil)	35%	1. 35
A 2% downhill slope*	10%	1. 10
A tailwind component of 10% of landing speed	20%	1. 20
Soft ground or snow*	25% or more	1. 25+

*Effect on ground roll will be proportionately greater

Cruise Performance

Cruise performance is affected by many things not least by the power setting and the use of mixture control. As seen earlier (in the carburettor section) in an extract from a cruise performance table, fuel consumption will vary enormously depending on the power setting used. Again it would be sensible to make a correction factor for fuel flow, due to flying an old aircraft and possible pilot inaccuracies in adjusting the mixture in accordance with the flight manual. As well as the cruise performance table illustrating the specific fuel consumption against altitude, temperature and power setting; the flight manual provides profile graphs for endurance and range. As with most things in life you don't get something for nothing. The faster you fly, the less distance you can cover and the shorter is the time that you can spend in the air on a given amount of fuel. The graphs show how far and for how long you could expect to fly at a given power setting at a particular altitude. I say "could expect" because of the factors that may affect the endurance or range. Factors, which the pilot should bear in mind and make sensible allowances for. One important piece of information that can seen in the cruise performance table is that varying the power from 2000 rpm to 2400 rpm can increase the fuel consumption by as much as 50% ! So with just this piece of knowledge, if you have to hold somewhere for whatever reason, do so at a sensible power setting that conserves fuel. You might need the time. In any event always plan to have enough fuel for your trip (factored for you and your aeroplane) to hold for at least 45 minutes and to get you to an alternative destination. The above performance calculations are only a personal suggestion and if you fly a at club or school you should consult their flying order book or the CFI recommendations for your aircraft.

Mass and Balance

Pre-amble and definition of terms

As mentioned in the performance section, the performance of an aircraft can be seriously affected if it is not loaded in the correct manner. That is, firstly ensure that the aircraft does not exceed the maximum authorised weight. Secondly, that the weight is distributed in such a way that the centre of gravity is retained within the prescribed limits set out in the flight manual. An aircraft operated in excess of its maximum authorised weight would display the following reduction in performance:

Higher takeoff speed
Longer takeoff run
Reduced rate of climb
Reduced service ceiling
Reduced cruise performance
Higher stalling speed
Increased landing speed
Increased landing run

To mention only the main items affected. Obviously, the greater the overload the greater the effect will become. Reflecting on AIC 67/2002 we can see a factor that could be applied for increased weight, but this does not mean that you can overload your aircraft so long as you factor in an adjustment for it! Maximum authorised weight, is, maximum authorised weight. As for balance, or the position of the C of G of an aircraft, this too will affect the aircraft in many ways. To the detriment of the handling qualities and performance if not located in the correct position. An aircraft loaded so as to have the C of G outside the forward limit will:

Require a large elevator down force to balance
Increase drag as a result
Increase stalling speed
Reduce cruise performance
Reduce nose pitch up available

If outside the rearward limit:
A spin would be more stable, therefore more difficult to recover
Reduce longitudinal stability
Aircraft would tend to pitch up, leading to possible stall on takeoff

These effects, as well as others, would contribute to make life very difficult for the unwary pilot. So it is crucial that as commander and person responsible, the pilot carry out the calculations necessary to ensure the aircraft is not over loaded and that the C of G is in an acceptable position. This is not only for performance reasons but legal as well. The pilot has a legal obligation to operate the aircraft within the manufacturers and regulatory bodies (e. g. CAA) limitations. If it is not, then the C of A will become invalid. Henceforth, following any incident that may occur the insurance company concerned may fail to pay up, leaving you liable for costs incurred. Following any accident, the weight and balance of the aircraft is likely to be one of the first things an accident investigator will check. Even, if at first, it did not appear to be a contributory factor it would still be a breach of the ANO and cause for the insurance company to discharge any claim. You also risk possible prosecution from the CAA. Avoiding all of this nastiness is really quite simple though, just complete a proper weight and balance check on the aircraft you intend to fly. As with the performance calculations, the best way to describe the process is by completing a sample weight and balance schedule.

Mass:

On the surface of the earth, weight is the resultant of the effect of earth's gravity on a particular mass. Therefore, as far as we are concerned they are one and the same thing.

Centre of Gravity (C of G):

Is that point through which the force of gravity can be considered to act on a body.

Moment:

A turning moment, commonly referred to as moment, is the resultant force of a mass multiplied by its distance from its turning point. If two people, of equal weight, sat on a seesaw at equal distances from the pivot, they would be in balance. The turning moments would be equal and opposite. We could also say that the centre of gravity of the seesaw was at the pivot point (ignoring the supporting structure). However, if either person moved or their weight changed then the balance would be disturbed and the position of the C of G would move. It is only by analysing the change in the turning moments (Mass × Distance) that we can calculate the new position of the C of G. The new balance point would indeed be our new centre of gravity position. Hence our interest in mass and balance.

Lever Arm:

Distance that a mass is removed from its pivot point. Used to calculate a moment.

Station:

Term sometimes used to describe lever arm.

Datum:

Vertical plane from which horizontal distances (lever arms) are measured.

Maximum Take-Off Weight:

Maximum weight approved for the start of the takeoff run.

Basic Empty Weight:

Weight of empty aircraft, including unusable fuel, full operating fluids, full engine oil. (Does not include disposable load or variable load).

Variable Load:

Pilot. (Minimum of one!).

Disposable Load:

Fuel, passengers and baggage.

The first item to work out is the actual weight of the loaded aircraft in the condition you intend to fly it. This requires the simple addition of the weight of the aircraft itself and all you intend putting into it. An example of this is also in the C152 flight manual, set out in tabular form, which is the traditional way. A sample table is illustrated below. Be careful when entering data as the units used vary. Being of American origin generally the flight manuals use imperial units of measure (i. e. pounds and inches). All calculations must be carried out using the same units and not a mix, then, converted if necessary at the end. In the example below we will use lbs and ins, as later we will see that these units are used in our sample flight manual centre of gravity envelope with which we will compare our figures. Some useful conversion figures are included at the end of the book should they be required. Entering the actual aircraft weight from the weighing schedule, the pilot and passenger weights, full fuel tank weight and a little baggage our table should look something like that shown below. Note every aircraft weight will be different and the actual weight of your aircraft must be used. Also, the relatively large baggage area is divided in two stations for weight and balance calculation purposes. Area one being the forward part and area two the rear part of the baggage shelf. Starting with the weights only, enter these into the table and calculate the total.

Sample Loading Table (Max AUW 1670 lbs)

Item	Weight (lbs)	Lever Arm (ins)	Moment (lbs x ins)
Basic a/c empty	1202. 0	29. 9	35940
Pilot	165. 0		
Passenger	165. 0		
Fuel (full)	147		
Baggage area 1	10		
Baggage area 2			
Total	1689		

Note, maximum baggage in area 1 is 120 lbs and area 2 is 40 lbs. Maximum total baggage 120 lbs.

The maximum authorised weight for the C152 is 1670 lbs. From the table the total reveals that this would be over weight by 19 lbs. So, unless pilot or passenger goes on a rather rapid diet and we leave the baggage behind, it demonstrates that we cannot take full fuel. Therefore, we need to reduce the fuel load by 19 lbs. This is a case where care needs to be taken to work in the correct units. Fuel weight can be taken as 7.2 lbs per Imp gal, 0.72 Kg per ltr or 6 lbs per US gal. As fuel is usually purchased in litres we will need to know how much is required in those units. Maximum usable fuel is 93 ltr, which corresponds to 147 lbs.

Therefore, the maximum fuel weight for this particular trip would be:

147 – 19 = 128 lbs

Converting lbs to Kgs: **128 lbs x 0.45359 = 58.06 Kgs**

Converting total fuel weight to ltrs:

58. 06 Kg ÷ 0.72 = 80.67 ltr (rounding down 80 ltr)

Therefore, the maximum usable fuel volume allowable in this case is 80.67 ltrs.

It is a useful exercise to calculate the maximum passenger weight that you can take with full fuel in the aircraft you regularly fly. In this particular case it would be:

Aircraft	1202. 0
Pilot	165. 0
Fuel	147. 0
Bag	10. 0
Total	1524. 0

Therefore, 1670 – 1524 = 146 lbs

With the weight corrected, the next thing to do is to enter a value for the lever arm of each of the weights in the table. These will be given by the manufacturer as a distance from an arbitrary datum, which in the C152 is the front face of the firewall. It is this distance that we will multiply by the relevant weight to arrive at its moment. Remember that this is only being done to provide us with a tool to calculate the ultimate C of G of the whole loaded aircraft. So, returning to our sample table and entering the revised weight for the fuel and the lever arms from the POH.

Sample Loading Table (Max AUW 1670lbs)

Item	Weight (lbs)	Lever Arm (ins)	Moment (lbs x ins)
Basic A/c empty	1202. 0	29. 9	35940
Pilot	165. 0	39. 0	6435
Passenger	165. 0	9. 0	6435
Fuel (80 ltr)	128	42. 17	5397
Baggage area 1	10	64. 0	640
Baggage area 2		84. 0	
Total	1670		54847

To calculate the centre of gravity (or lever arm) of the loaded aircraft divide the total moment by the total weight:

54847 ÷ 1670 = 32.84 ins

We now need to check that this is within the permitted range by plotting the information on the centre of gravity limits or moment envelope graphs.

Using the total weight and C of G position we can see that the aircraft is within the envelope outlined on the graph and therefore safe to fly.

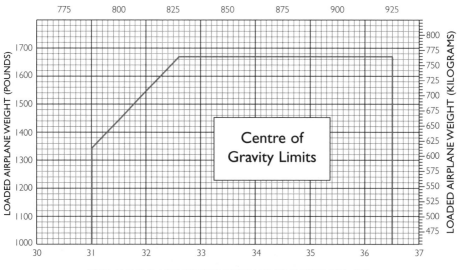

AIRPLANE C.G. LOCATION-INCHES AFT OF DATUM (STA. 0.0)

If the C of G had proven to be outside the limits then we would have to consider ways in which to get it back inside the envelope. Which would entail moving the position of, or changing a particular weight. Although this is unlikely to be a problem with two average people in the C152, it is possible.

With the information available in the C152 flight manual it is possible to obtain values for the moment of each station directly from the loading graph, shown below. Together with the centre of gravity moment envelope, removes the need to fill in a loading table. To use the loading simply enter the weight of a particular station on the vertical axis, plot across to the appropriate reference line (e. g. pilot and passenger) then vertically down to read off the moment.

This effectively carries out the multiplication done in the table.

Loading Graph

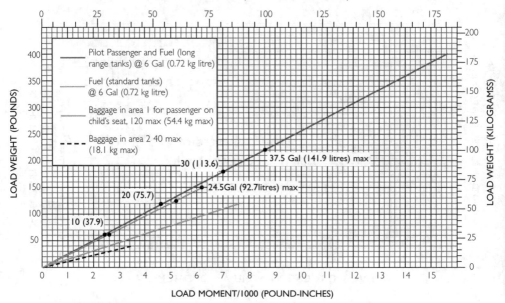

NOTES: Line representing adjustable seats shows the pilot or passenger centre of gravity on adjustable seats positioned for an average occupant. Refer to the Loading Arrangements Diagram for forward and aft limits of occupant CG range.

The moments obtained from this graph are added together as they are in the table above to obtain a total moment. Then using the centre of gravity moment envelope graph in the manual and reproduced below, enter the total weight on the vertical axis and plot horizontally across at that weight. Then plot up from the horizontal axis at the value of the total moment. The lines need to meet within the envelope for the aircraft to be correctly loaded. Note when using this graph the total value for the moments has been divided by 1000 to keep the numbers small.

Centre of Gravity Moment Envelope

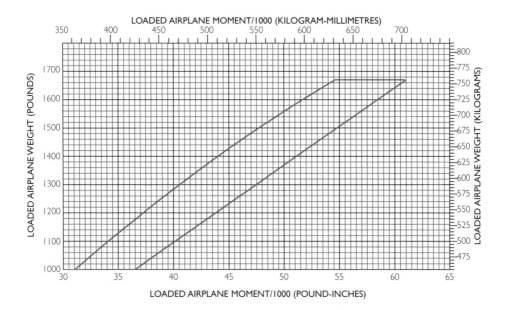

LOADED AIRPLANE MOMENT/1000 (KILOGRAM-MILLIMETRES)

LOADED AIRPLANE WEIGHT (POUNDS)

LOADED AIRPLANE WEIGHT (KILOGRAMS)

LOADED AIRPLANE MOMENT/1000 (POUND-INCHES)

Using the loading graph is a lot quicker but a little less accurate, so if in doubt, recheck using a table and calculation method to be on the safe side. Any of the forgoing is only an example and not for operational use. Always use the flight manual information that applies to your particular aircraft for calculations, as each one will vary from another similar C152. The weight and balance schedule will normally be provided by the maintenance organisation responsible for the aircraft and be inserted in the flight manual. One major difference between C152's is the long-range tank version. Other minor weight variations can occur due to differing levels of radio equipment fitted. For those of you that are a bit wizard on a computer and are familiar with Excel or similar, you can reporduce the weight and balance graphs in these programs and plot direectly on to hem letting the computer do the work! Nothing like plastic brains eh! But beware, garbage in, garbage out!

Typical Speeds and Limitations

Take–Off	Rotate		50 kts
	(Soft field 45 kts)		
Climb	Best rate (Vy)	zero flap	65 kts
	"	10 deg flap	60 kts
	Best angle (Vx)	zero flap	60 kts
	"	10 deg flap	54 kts
	Cruise climb		75 kts
Cruise	Normal 2200/2300 rpm		90 kts
	Safe slow 2000/2100 20 flap		70 kts
Glide	Best range (0 flap)		65 kts
	Best endurance (0 flap)		55 kts
Approach	Normal		65 kts (Vat 60)
	Glide		65 kts (Vat 60)
	Flapless		70 kts (Vat 65)
	Short Field (Full flap)		60 kts (Vat 55)

In strong winds and turbulence it would be advisable to add 5 kts to the take-off and landing speeds and consider reducing flap settings.

Maximum demonstrated crosswind   12 Kts

To calculate crosswind component either use the table below or the method described earlier, using the imaginary watch face.

Crosswind angle	10	20	30	40	50	60	70	80	90
Crosswind factor	0. 2	0. 3	0. 5	0. 6	0. 7	0. 8	0. 9	0. 9	1. 0

Maximum Airspeeds

Maximum Speed Permitted (Vne)	149 kts
Maximum Structural Cruising Speed (Vno)	111 kts
Maximum Manoeuvring Speed (Va)	104 kts
Maximum Speed Flaps Extended (Vfe)	85 kts
Maximum Authorised Take off Weight (MATW)	1670 lbs

Stall Speeds (Indicated airspeeds given in knots)

1. At MATW with centre of gravity in the most rearward position and idle power.

Flap Deflection	Angle of Bank			
	0°	30°	45°	60°
Up	36	39	43	51
10°	36	39	43	51
30°	31	33	37	44

2. At MATW with centre of gravity in the most forward position and idle power.

Flap Deflection	Angle of Bank			
	0°	30°	45°	60°
Up	40	43	48	57
10°	40	43	48	57
30°	35	38	42	49

Airspeed Indicator Colour Coding

Red line Vne	149 kts
Yellow arc (caution range)	111-149 kts
Green arc (normal operating range)	40 – 111 kts
White arc (flap operating range)	35 – 85 kts

Structural Load Limitations

Maximum positive load factor:

Flaps up	4. 4 g
Flaps down	3. 5 g

Maximum negative:

Flaps up	-1. 76 g
Flaps down	0

Flight by Night
The aircraft is approved for flight by night.   Providing the minimum equipment for flight at night (see ANO, schedule 5) is serviceable.

Flight in Icing Conditions
Flight in icing conditions is strictly prohibited.

Other useful figures

Typical engine Avco Lycoming 0-235-L2C:
110 hp @ 2550 rpm
Max. RPM 2550 (Red line)

Oil capacity:
6 US quarts (5.7 ltr)
Min. safe 4 US quarts (3. 8 ltr)

Oil temperature:
Max. 118°C/245F (red line)
Normal range 100F –245F(Green arc)

Oil Pressure:
Max. 115 psi (Red line)
Normal range 60-90 psi (Green arc)
Min. idling 25 psi (Red line)

Fuel Capacity:

Standard Tanks	Usable Fuel	24. 5 US gals (93 ltr)
Long Range	Usable Fuel	37. 5 US gals (142 ltr)

Some Typical Performance Figures

Based on a hypothetical standard day with zero wind. Aircraft in good flying condition with no account taken for pilot technique or surface conditions for take off or landing.

Figures only approximate and unfactored (refer to performance section). Therefore appropriate allowances should be made for operational use.

Take off:	Ground run	221 m
	Take off distance	408 m
Landing:	Ground run	145 m
	Landing distance	366 m
Speeds:	Maximum at sea level	110 kts
	Typical cruise (63% pwr, 4000 ft)	95 kts
Rate of Climb:	At 1000 ft (66 kts)	675 fpm

Service Ceiling: 14,700 ft

Glide: At 60 kts, flaps up, zero wind. Approx 1.5 nm/1000 ft

Tyre pressures:	Nose	30 psi (2.1 bar)
	Mains	21 psi (1.45 bar)

Cessna 152 Pre – Flight Check List

Check lists are an essential part of a pilot's equipment, and their importance cannot be over emphasised. Whilst in flight checks should be committed to memory, as these are relatively few, the checks required before getting airborne should rigorously follow the approved check list. Never rush the checks, work at your own pace steadily through each line in the check list. Also, beware of any line in a check list that has more than one item, as the second item can easily be missed and subsequently not checked; especially if you feel under pressure to get the job done. The checks actually begin before you get to the aircraft. First of all check that all the paperwork is in order and that the aircraft has enough hours left for your flight before the next service check. With that done and the correct flight authorisation complete, on approaching the aircraft take a distant view of the way it is parked and how it appears to stand on the ground. Does it stand level? Does list to one side or perhaps looks rather nose low. Either may be due to the terrain it is parked on or indicate some other problem. If parked on soft ground (e. g. grass in winter time) it may have sunk in a bit and it would be prudent to push the aircraft forward out of the depressions before attempting to taxi. Also make a note of the condition of the area in which you intend to taxi if it is a grass surface, which can obscure all manner of nasty surprises for the unwary! Rabbit holes, old tie down left behind, even ill placed taxiway lights seem to have an amazingly magnetic attraction to an aircraft when you get distracted by your passenger or some one else wittering at you through the headset. With this in mind we can begin with our more detailed checks.

Ensure that any tie downs, external control locks, wheel chocks and pitot cover are removed and stored securely.

Aircraft tie down point on wing strut.

Any ice or frost must be removed from all surfaces. Special care should be taken with the Perspex windows as these can be damaged very easily. Do not use a credit card scraper!

Using the numbered plan view as guide, follow the rest of the pre flight check list.

External Check List

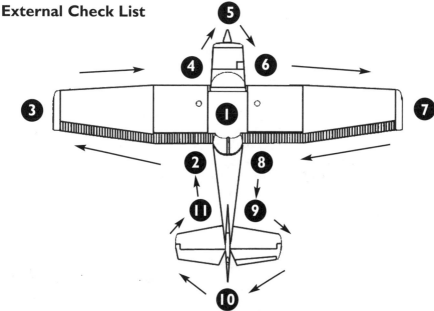

1.   In Cabin:

(a)   Remove control lock and stow in glove box.
(b)   Magnetos off and key out.
(c)   Park brake on.
(d)   Check all radios and all other electrical equipment is switched off.
(e)   Master switch on: check fuel gauges rising (note contents indicated)
(f)   Turn on: Anti-collision beacon
                  Pitot heater
                  Navigation lights
                  Landing lights
(g)   Check all items switched on for serviceability in turn. (pitot will take a short while to warm up so check this last).
(h)   Return to cockpit.
(i)   Turn off electrical equipment listed above. Lower Flaps (20).
(j)   Master switch off.
(k)   Check First Aid kit sealed and secure
        (If not sealed a vital part might be missing).

(l)   Check fire extinguisher secure and pressure reading in green arc.

(m)   Close cabin door and check door and window security.

(k)   Proceed around aircraft in clockwise direction.

2. Port Undercarriage:

(a)   **Security and condition of brake calliper and pads.**
Calliper is semi-floating type so will have a certain amount of
play when checked.

(b)   **Pads** should not be worn down to metal backing plate.

(c)   **Security and condition of brake disc.** Should not be loose,
rusty or pitted.

(d)   **Hydraulic lines.** Check for damage and leaks, particularly adjacent
to the calliper.

(e)   **Condition of wheel and tyre.** Check for general wear, damage,
alignment of creep marks and correct inflation.

(f)   **Leg and Fairing.** Check general condition, particularly security of wheel
fairing and if conditions are conducive, check for mud filling the fairing.

3. Port Wing:

(a)   **Lower Wing Surface.** Check for any damage and inspection panels
security. Operate fuel drain valve into appropriate container; check for
dirt, water and correct colour, repeat if necessary. (First flight of day and after
refuelling). After use ensure that fuel drain is closed and not dripping.

(b)   **Port Flap.** Check for any damage, drain holes clear, linkage free, all nuts
secure, runners greased. (Should be a small amount of play when the flap is
handled)

(c)   **Port Aileron.** Check full and free movement, condition and security
of hinges, split pins, linkage and mass balance. Drain holes clear. Aileron
should be smooth in movement requiring little force. Take care with
fingers inside the hinge line when checking operation. (Prevent movement
with other hand).

(d)   **Wing Tip.** Check for any damage, security and navigation light (red).

(e)   Leading edge. Check for any damage, pitot tube and fuel vent clear.
Check stall warner. Cabin air vent clear.

(f)   **Port Strut.** Check for any damage and security.

(g)   **Upper Wing Surface.** Check for any damage. Visually check fuel
contents and compare with fuel gauge readings. Check fuel filler cap
secure. (When checking upper wing surface only stand on the footplate fitted to the
strut, if no such plate is fitted use a stepladder)

4. Port Cowling:

(a) Check static vent clear.

(b) Check windscreen clean and undamaged.

5. Front of Engine:

(a) **Nose Wheel.** Security of nuts and split pins, state of tyre. Freedom of operating linkage. Oleo extension, at least 3 inches. No oil leaks. Shimmy damper serviceable and secure.

(b) **Propeller.** Treat live at all times. Check for cracks or nicks especially along the leading edge and spinner for condition and security. DO NOT TURN THE PROPELLER.

(c) **Front of Cowling.** Carburettor air intake and filter clear. General condition of baffles and cylinders that can be seen. Cowling secure. Condition and security of landing light. Check oil cooler clear and no leaks. Security of alternator and belt.

6. Starboard Cowling:

(a) **Check security** and see if any screws are loose or missing.

(b) Open inspection cover, remove dipstick and check oil level (min 4 qts).

(c) Replace dipstick finger tight only. Operate fuel strainer drain into fuel tester container, check for dirt, water and correct colour. After use ensure that fuel drain is closed and not dripping.

(d) **Secure inspection cover.**

(e) **Check cabin air intake.**

(f) **Check exhaust pipes secure** only when engine cold.

7. Starboard Wing:

(a) **Upper Wing Surface.** Check for any damage. Visually check fuel contents and compare with fuel gauge readings. Check fuel filler cap secure. (When checking upper wing surface only stand on the footplate fitted to the strut, if no such plate is fitted use a stepladder).

(b) **Lower Wing Surface.** Check for any damage and inspection panels security. Operate fuel drain valve into appropriate container; check for dirt, water and correct colour, repeat if necessary. (First flight of day and after refuelling). After use ensure that fuel drain is closed and not dripping.

(c) **Leading Edge.** Check for any damage. Cabin air vent clear.

(d) **Starboard Strut.** Check for any damage and security.

(e) **Wing Tip.** Check for any damage, security and navigation light (green).

(f)   **Starboard Aileron.** Check full and free movement, condition and security of hinges, split pins, linkage and mass balance. Drain holes clear. Aileron should be smooth in movement requiring little force. Take care with fingers inside the hinge line when checking operation. (Prevent movement with other hand).

(g)   **Starboard Flap.** Check for any damage, drain holes clear, linkage free, all nuts secure, runners greased.

8. Starboard Undercarriage:

(a)   **Security and condition of brake calliper and pads.** Calliper is semi-floating type so will have a certain amount of play when checked. Pads should not be worn down to metal backing plate.

(b)   **Security and condition of brake disc.** Should not be loose, rusty or pitted.

(c)   **Hydraulic lines.** Check for damage and leaks, particularly adjacent to the calliper.

(d)   **Condition of wheel and tyre.** Check for general wear, damage, alignment of creep marks and correct inflation.

(e)   **Leg and Fairing.** Check general condition, particularly security of wheel fairing and if conditions are conducive, check for mud filling the fairing.

9. Starboard Fuselage:

(a)   Condition of rear window and check clean.

(b)   Check upper, lower and sides surfaces of fuselage for any damage.

(c)   Check drain holes clear.

(d)   Check ADF wire aerial if fitted.

10. Tail Unit:

(a)   **Starboard Tail Plane.** Check upper and lower surfaces for any damage, inspection panels secure.

(b)   **Starboard Elevator.** Check full and free movement, check secure and undamaged, linkage free. Drain holes clear. Use care when checking movement.

(c)   **Trim Tab.** Check trim (holding elevator only) for damage, operation and security.

(d)   **Tail Fin.** Check secure and undamaged and fairings. Check beacon and aerial attachment.

(e)   **Rudder.** Surface undamaged. Hinge bolts secure, control linkages secure, turnbuckles wired, full and free movement of control. Check navigation light (white). When moving rudder do so gently and do no touch rudder trim tab. Check tail tie down eye.

(f)   **Port Elevator and Tail Plane.** Check as for starboard side. (Note trim tab only on starboard side).

11. Port Fuselage:

(a)   Condition of rear window and check clean.

(b)   Check upper, lower and sides surfaces of fuselage for any damage.

(c)   Check any other aerials not previously checked.

Internal Checks

1. Seat	Adjusted and secure.
2. Harness	Lap and shoulder strap adjusted and secure.
3. Doors and Windows	Check security.
4. Parking Brake	On.
5. Instruments	Undamaged, legible and secure.
6. Cabin air/heat	Free movement of controls and set closed.
7. Fuel	On.
8. Circuit Breakers	Check all in.
9. Trim	Check full and free movement, in correct sense and set for take off.
10. Controls	Full and free movement in correct sense.
11. Mixture	Full and free movement. Set to fully rich.
12. Throttle	Full and free movement. Set to ¼" open.
13. Carb Heat Control	Full and free movement. Set to cold.
14. Primer	Prime as required and lock.
15. Master Switch	On. (If night nav lights on).
16. Radios	Off. (Unless start up clearance or airfield data reqd. Ensure off for start up).
17. Altimeter	Set as required. (Aerodrome QNH if departing, QFE for circuit, if setting not obtained set to zero should show anticipated QFE, set to airfield elevation the QNH, both +50, -75ft).
18. Beacon	On.

Starting

1. LOOKOUT	Check all round aircraft, open window, shout clear prop. Cover brakes. (Park brake notoriously unreliable)
2. Magneto	Key in, (hand on throttle) turn to start position.

After Start

1. Starter Warner Light   Out, if not, immediately turn the magneto switch to stop the engine.
2. Oil Pressure   Rising to green arc within 30 secs (If not, mag switch off).
3. RPM   Set 1200 rpm as normal idle engine speed.
4. Ammeter   Check holding positive charge.
5. Suction   Check 3" to 5" (green arc).
6. Radios   On and tuned to correct frequencies. (Obtain ATIS or airfield data). Check intercom function adjust if necessary.
7. Instruments   Set D.I. and Alt. Check A.I. erected. Turn Co-ord. flag away.
8. Flaps   Check last stage down then all stages up (symmetrical).
9. Magnetos   Dead cut check at 1200 rpm. (Looking for a drop no stop, if engine is still cold it may not run particularly smoothly on one mag at this stage)
10. Radio   Turn up volume and listen out. Request radio check and (if required) taxi clearance.

Taxying

1. Brakes   Close throttle, release brakes. Increase power sufficiently to move forward then close throttle and gently test brakes. (If brakes fail to release see brake section for further info).
2. Rudder   Check directional control.
3. Instruments   During turns check compass and D.I. turning correctly and in same direction. Turn co-ordinator showing a turn in the correct direction and the ball a skid.
4. Wind direction   Note the wind direction relative to taxi direction and hold the control column in the appropriate position. Be aware of weathercock action in strong crosswind.

Power Checks

1. Position   Into wind, clear of rough ground, loose stones, personnel and other aircraft. Also that subsequent propwash will not adversely affect other a/c especially tail wheel types.
2. Brakes   On, but covered as well.
3. Oil   Temperature and pressure steady and within limits.
4. Rpm   Check clear all round. Set to 1700.

5. Carb Heat		Operate to hot position, should show approx 50-75 rpm drop, return to cold position.
6. Magnetos		Check each magneto in turn. Max permissible drop 125 rpm, max differential is 50 rpm. Ensure after check mags on both.
7. Suction		Between 4. 5 and 5. 4"Hg or in the green arc
8. Ammeter		Charging (i. e. positive indication).
9. Oil		Temperature and pressure steady and within limits.
10. Idle		Smoothly close the throttle and check rpm 500-700. Recheck oil temp. and pressure as above. Ammeter discharging (i. e. negative indication)
11. Rpm		Reset to 1200.

Pre Take Off Checks

1.	T	Trim control set for take off.
2.	T	Throttle friction nut finger tight.
3.	M	Mixture rich.
4.	C	Carb Heat cold. (Recheck if take off delayed).
5.	M	Master switch on.
6.	M	Magnetos on both.
7.	F	Fuel on and sufficient.
8.	P	Primer in and locked.
9.	F	Flaps as required.
10.	G	Gauges, oil temp and pressure in limits.
11.	I	Instruments, D. I. set Alt. set.
12.	R	Radios, set as required.
13.	H	Harnesses secure.
14.	H	Hatches, doors and windows secure.
15.	P	Pitot heat, as required.
16.	C	Controls, all full and free movement.
17.	T	Take off brief. Review speeds. Assess crosswind effect and control reqd. Establish emergency procedures.

Take Off - ## <u>Normal Take off</u>

1. Lookout
2. Line up

3. Brakes
4. Throttle
5. Oil
6. Airspeed

Obtain clearance, check approach path clear visually.
On runway centre line, ensure nosewheel straight.
Check D. I. indicating runway heading
Off, heels on the floor.
Smoothly open to full power, check at least 2350 rpm.
Temperature and pressure steady in green arc.
Increasing at 50 kts use elevator raise nose. Lift off at 55 kts
Climb at 65 kts (clean). 60 kts with flap.

After Take Off

1. Lookout

2. Flaps
3. Oil
4. Departure

Point selected left of nose. Check drift!
Maintain any noise abatement procedure.
Retract above 200 ft, not below 60 kts.
Temperature and pressure steady and within limits.
As per ATC instructions or brief.

Climb - ## <u>Normal Climb</u>

1. Airspeed
2. Throttle
3. Mixture

Clean 65 kts for best rate of climb.
Full open.
Full rich below 3000 ft.

En-route Climb

1. Airspeed
2. Throttle
3. Mixture

75 Kts.
Full open.
Full rich below 3000 ft.

Cruise

1.	Airspeed	80-100 kts (dependent on power set, alt etc).
2.	Power	2000 – 2400 rpm (check cruise perf table, normal 2250).
3.	Elevator trim	Adjust as required.
4.	Mixture	Lean as per recommendations.

En-route Checks:

FREDA

1.	**F**	Fuel – check contents.
2.	**R**	Radios – Com. Check volume.
		Change frequency if reqd.
		Nav. Check freq and ident as reqd.
3.	**E**	Engine – Check for carb icing.
		Check oil temperature and pressure.
		Ammeter charging.
		Suction within limits.
		Mixture as reqd.
4.	**D**	D. I. – Synchronised with compass
5.	**A**	Altimeter – Set as required

Pre Stall, Spin or Aerobatic Checks:

HASELL

1.	**H**	Height - sufficient to recover by 2500 ft a.g.l.
2.	**A**	Airframe - flaps as required for stalling (no flap for spins or aerobatics)
		Brakes off.
3.	**S**	Security - doors, windows and harness secure.
		No loose articles. Check fire extinguisher fastened in place.
4.	**E**	Engine - check oil temperature and pressure.
		Mixture as required.
		Clear any carb ice.
		Check fuel contents
5.	**L**	Location – check clear of:

	A	–	Active airfields
	B	–	Built up areas
	C	–	Cloud or controlled airspace
	D	–	Danger areas

6.	**L**	LOOKOUT – carry out a 180° or two 90° turns to check no other aircraft around or below.

Between successive manoeuvres (e. g. stalls) the **HELL** elements of the check are normally sufficient.

Note: reset DI following the completion of the exercise.

On approach to an airfield carry out a **FREDA** check, setting mixture to rich and Altimeter to QFE when field is in sight.

Pre Landing:

BUMPFICHH

1.	**B**	Brakes – Off, pressure check
2.	**U**	Undercarriage – Fixed
3.	**M**	Mixture – Rich
4.	**P**	Propeller – Pitch fixed
5.	**F**	Fuel – On and sufficient for "Go Around".
6.	**I**	Instruments – Engine gauges normal
		Altimeter set (QFE)
		DI set
7.	**C**	Carb Heat – Check for icing then return to cold.
8.	**H**	Harnesses – Check pilot and passenger.
9.	**H**	Hatches – Check doors and windows secure.

Landing:

Normal Landing

1.	Carb heat	Apply full heat before reducing power.
2.	Flaps	Select 20° when speed is below 85 kts.
3.	Airspeed	Adjust attitude for 65 kts and trim.
		Reduce to 60 kts at the threshold.
4.	Touchdown	Hold off to touchdown on main wheels first, then lower nose wheel gently.
5.	Braking	Minimum required for runway length.

Flapless Landing:

1.	Airspeed	70 kts
2.	Braking	More braking may be required due to higher landing speed.

Shortfield Landing:

1.	Flaps	Full flap on final approach - 30°∞
2.	Airspeed	60 kts (54 kts at threshold)
3.	Touchdown	Main wheels first, lower nose wheel promptly.
4.	Braking	Apply positively (beware of wheel lock).

Glide Approach:

1. Airspeed	Flaps up	65 kts
	Flaps 20°	65 kts
	Flaps 30°	60 kts

Notes: *During prolonged glides the engine should be warmed every 500 ft. The approach speeds are for calm conditions, in gusty or turbulent conditions the speeds should be increased accordingly.*

Go- Around (overshoot)

1. Throttle	Full power (control pitch and yaw)
2. Carb Heat	Select cold position.
3. Airspeed	Adjust attitude for 60 kts.
4. Flaps	If 30°, retract to 20° as soon as possible. Retract remaining 20° when above 200 ft and positive rate of climb.
5. Radio	Inform ATC.

After Landing

Taxi clear of runway and stop the aircraft.

1. Carb Heat	Cold.
2. Flaps	Up.
3. Pitot heat	Off.
4. Throttle	Throttle friction nut loose.
5. Lights	Strobe and landing lights off.
6. Transponder	Standby.
7. Other electrics	Non-essentials off.

Shut Down

1. Park   Into wind, nosewheel straight.
2. Parking brake   On
3. Engine   Idle for at least 30secs at 1200, check oil temperature and pressure.
4. Magnetos   Dead cut check.
5. Radios   Com and nav off.
6. Mixture   Lean to I. C. O.

After Engine Stops:

7. Magnetos   OFF
8. Beacon   Off
9. Nav lights   Off
10. Master switch   OFF, key out.
11. Fuel   Left on in C152
12. Control lock   Fit in place
13. Harnesses   Left tidy
14. External   Pitot cover on.
                      Secure windows and doors.
                      Tie down and/or fit chocks if necessary.

EMERGENCIES

Fire on the Ground - Before Engine Start

1. Continue cranking for the time required for the rest of procedure.
2. Mixture ----------------------- I. C. O.
3. Fuel ------------------------------ OFF
4. Master Switch --------------- OFF
4. Magnetos --------------------- OFF
5. Exit aircraft with fire extinguisher and direct contents onto base of fire.

After Engine Start

Run the engine at 1700 rpm in an attempt to suck any flames into the engine for a short time (20 secs). Then shut down.

1. Mixture .... I. C. O.
2. Fuel ----------------------------- OFF
3. Master switch .... OFF
4. Magnetos .... OFF
5. Exit aircraft with fire extinguisher and direct contents onto base of fire.

Fire in the Air

Engine Fire

1. Mixture .... I. C. O
2. Fuel ---------------------------- OFF
3. Mayday Call
4. Master switch .... OFF
5. Cabin heat and air .... OFF (except upper air vents)
6. Throttle .... Closed
7. Magnetos .... OFF
8. Speed .... 85 kts (Or faster if required to extinguish flames)
9. Side slip if necessary to keep flame and smoke away from cabin.
10. Carry out forced landing procedure.

Cabin Fire

1. Master switch .... OFF
2. Air vents .... Closed
3. Fire Extinguisher .... Use if necessary, but then ventilate cabin well.
4. Land as soon as possible.

Electrical Fire

1. Master switch .... OFF
2. All other switches (except ignition) Off
3. Air vents .... Closed
4. Fire Extinguisher .... Use if necessary, but then ventilate cabin well.

If fire appears to be out and electrical power is required
5. Master switch .... ON
6. Circuit breakers .... Check, do not reset any that have tripped.
7. Electrics Switch on one circuit at a time carefully, try to identify each one as safe before proceeding to the next.

Engine Failure After Take Off

1. Lower nose to maintain best gliding speed
2. Close throttle
3. Select the most suitable landing area ahead or around the aircraft bearing in mind the wind direction and any obstacles
4. Use flap as necessary
5. Mixture .... I. C. O
6. Fuel .... OFF
7. Magnetos .... OFF
8. Mayday call if time permits
9. Master .... OFF
10. Harness .... Tight, unlatch doors.

Forced Landing without Power

1. Adopt glide attitude and trim for correct glide speed.
2. Assess wind velocity.
3. Select a landing area.
4. Establish 1000 ft area and plan descent.
5. Carry out engine failure checks: Fuel on and sufficient
   Mixture rich
   Throttle set
   Carb heat check and change position
   Magnetos on both
   Primer locked

If no obvious fault found that will rectify situation.

6. Mayday call (A/c call sign, position and route most important)
7. Complete committal drill:

> Mixture I. C. O.
> Fuel off
> Throttle closed
> Magnetos off
> Brakes off
> Harness tight
> Doors unlatched
> Master switch off (when electrics are finished with)

8. Recheck approach to landing area and adjust as necessary.
9. Use full flap for touchdown if not already fully down.
10 After touchdown stop as soon as possible with heavy braking.

Forced Landing with Power

1. Assess the time available and check:

> Fuel state
> Hours of daylight remaining
> Rate of weather deterioration

2. Assess wind velocity.
3. Select suitable landing area
4. Carry out an inspection run at slow safe cruising speed (70 kts, flap 20°) initially at around 500 ft a. g. l. to for check obstructions.
5. Carry out further inspection run at around 100 ft for closer check of approach path and surface condition (if time and conditions permit).
6. Approach using short field technique.
7. After touchdown stop as soon as possible with heavy braking.

Ditching Procedure

1. Set up minimum rate of descent (55 kts).
2. Mayday call.
3. Head towards any shipping.
4. Harness tight.
5. Secure or jettison heavy objects.
6. Unlatch doors and windows.
7. Activate E. L. B.
8. If large swell and light wind, land along swell in tail down near stalling attitude. If strong wind and light or heavy swell, land into wind in tail down near stalling attitude.
9. Evacuate aircraft and DO NOT inflate life jackets until outside cabin.

Action in event of Radio Failure

1. Check frequency is correct.
2. Check volume setting.
3. Check microphone and headset plugs are in and secure.
4. Adjust squelch setting (if applicable)
5. Check circuit breaker (reset only once).
6. Transmit blind or use PTT switch to try and communicate.

Use appropriate non-radio procedures and obey visual signals. If unaware of exact procedure in circuit, keep clear of other traffic and on final approach flash landing light on and off. Land unless given signal not to.

Electrical Failure

1. Check circuit breaker not tripped (reset only once).
2. Check master switch on.
3. Assess nature of failure (i. e. one circuit of little significance or major that may lead to total electrical failure).
4. If second scenario then reduce electrical load.
5. Notify ATC.
6. Land as soon as practicable.

If all electrics are lost then see above for radio failure.

Low Voltage Light Illuminated (or minus ammeter reading).

1. Turn alternator part of master switch off for a couple of seconds, then back on.
2. If light comes remains on, reduce electrical load as much as possible.
3. Consider switching off master switch when electrics not required,
   (will not affect function of engine).
4. Notify ATC
5. Land as soon as practicable.

   Note: The light may come on at low rpm, but should go
           out when the rpm is increased (see electrical section).

Appendix 1

Glossary of Terms

Some Common V Codes:

Va	–	**Manoeuvring Speed**
		This is the maximum speed at which you should make any abrupt or full control movements.
Vno	–	**Maximum Structural Cruising Speed**
		This is the maximum speed at which you can fly in turbulent conditions.
Vne	–	**Never Exceed Speed**
		This is the maximum speed that you may fly in any circumstances and must not be exceeded.
Vfe	–	**Maximum Speed with Flaps Extended**
		This is the highest speed allowed to extend the flaps or fly with them extended.
Vs1	–	**Stalling Speed in clean configuration (ie flaps up) and idle power**
Vs0	–	**Stalling Speed with full flap and idle power.**
Vx	–	**Best Angle of Climb**
		This is the speed at which there will be the greatest gain in altitude in a given horizontal distance.
Vy	–	**Best Rate of Climb.**
		This is the speed at which there will be the greatest gain in altitude in a given time.

Airspeeds

IAS	–	**Indicated Airspeed** This is the speed displayed on the airspeed indicator and normally expressed in knots.
RAS	–	**Rectified Airspeed** This is the IAS corrected for instrument and the position of the static vent.
TAS	–	**True Airspeed** This is RAS corrected for density.

Appendix 2.

Common Abbreviations

AAIB	Air accident investigation branch
A. G. L.	Above ground level
AIC	Aeronautical information circular
ADF	Automatic direction finding.
ANO	Air navigation order
ATC	Air traffic control
BHP	Brake horsepower
CAA	Civil aviation authority
CofG	Centre of Gravity.
CofR	Certificate of Registration
CofA	Certificate of Airworthiness
CofMR	Certificate of Maintenance Review
CofRS	Certificate of Release to Service
DME	Distance measuring equipment.
E. L. B.	Emergency locator beacon.
ICO	Idle cut off.
IFR	Instrument flight rules
MSL	Mean sea level.
POH	Pilots operating handbook.
QFE	Barometric pressure set on altimeter to read height above a datum.
QNH	Barometric pressure set on altimeter to read altitude above MSL
SAE	Society of automobile engineers.
VHF	Very high frequency.
VFR	Visual flight rules

Appendix 3

International Standard Atmosphere (ISA)
Conditions at Sea Level:

Temperature	+15°C
Density	1225 gm/ccm
Pressure	1013 Hpa (or mb)
Lapse Rate	1. 98°C/1000 ft

Useful Conversion Factors:
Distances
Centimetres to inches	×	0.3937
Inches to centimetres	×	2. 54
Metres to feet	×	3. 2808
Feet to metres	×	0. 3048
Kilometres to nautical miles	×	0. 5399
Nautical miles to kilometres	×	1. 852

Weights
Kilograms to pounds	×	2. 2046
Pounds to kilograms	×	0. 4536

Volumes
Litres to imperial gallons	×	0. 22
Litres to US gallons	×	0. 264
Imperial gallons to litres	×	4. 546
Imperial gallons to US gallons	×	1. 201
US gallons to litres	×	3. 785
US gallons to imperial gallons	×	0. 833

Other Terms:
Dihedral	Wings that incline upwards from mounting point to wing tip.
Wash out	Slight twist in a wing that reduces angle of incidence towards the tip.
Creep	Movement of tyre around the rim of the wheel, can cause the valve to tear off the inner tube.

Notes

Notes